GOSPEL ABOVE ALL

1 Corinthians 15:3

J. D. GREEAR

LifeWay Press®
Nashville, Tennessee

STUDENT MINISTRY PUBLISHING TEAM

Director, Student Ministry
BEN TRUEBLOOD

Content Editor
DREW DIXON

Manager, Student
Ministry Publishing
JOHN PAUL BASHAM

Content Specialist
STEPHANIE LIVENGOOD

Graphic Designer
SARAH SPERRY

Editorial Team Leader
KAREN DANIEL

Published by LifeWay Press® • © 2019 J. D. Greear

ISBN 978-1-5359-0086-7 • Item 005803190

Dewey decimal classification: 230
Subject headings: GOSPEL / CHRISTIANITY / CHURCH

Scripture quotations are taken from the Christian Standard Bible®, Copyright © 2017 by Holman Bible Publishers. Used by permission. Christian Standard Bible® and CSB® are federally registered trademarks of Holman Bible Publishers.

To order additional copies of this resource, write to LifeWay Resources Customer Service; One LifeWay Plaza; Nashville, TN 37234; email orderentry@lifeway.com; order online at LifeWay.com; fax 615-251-5933; call toll free 800-458-2772; or visit the LifeWay Christian Store serving you.

Printed in the United States of America

Student Ministry Publishing • LifeWay Resources
One LifeWay Plaza • Nashville, TN 37234

CONTENTS

HOW TO USE THIS STUDY

Welcome! We hope this eight week journey through the Gospels will lead you and your Student Ministry to a gospel revolution. Here's how the study works.

GROUP

Start. Your actual group session will most likely begin here with an icebreaker designed to help you ease into the study and get everyone talking. A brief description of J.D.'s teaching helps set the stage for hearing from God during each video teaching session.

Watch. Key statements from the video session are provided so you can follow along and take notes as J.D. and his guests discuss the content.

Discuss. These questions help the group study Scripture passages that reinforce J.D.'s teaching on the video. Each question is designed to lead the group deeper into the gospel so the gospel becomes foundational in members' lives. These questions facilitate the work the Holy Spirit is accomplishing in the lives of individuals and the group.

Respond. These gospel exercises allow group members to enjoy a smaller group experience, which increases the likelihood that everyone's voice will be heard. Although some of these activities introduce further opportunities for Bible study, some focus on prayer, meditation, and encouragement.

Prayer. This section ends the group time with some practical handles and pointers for prayer.

PERSONAL EXPERIENCE

Personal Study. Each week features two personal studies to go deeper into the truths of the week's topic.

Engage with your community. These exercises are meant to help you connect more deeply with your church community.

Engage with the world. These exercises are meant to help you connect more deeply with those who have not yet believed in Jesus.

TIPS FOR LEADING A SMALL GROUP

Introduction. Pray for each meeting beforehand. Ask the Holy Spirit to work through you and the group discussion as you point to Jesus each week through God's Word.

Everyone Participates. Encourage everyone to ask questions, share responses, or read aloud.

No One Dominates. Be sure your time speaking as a leader takes up less than half your time together as a group. Politely guide discussion if anyone begins to dominate the discussion.

Don't Rush. Don't feel that a moment of silence is a bad thing. People often need time to think about their responses to questions they've just heard or to gain courage to share what God is stirring in their hearts.

Affirm and Follow Up on Input. Make sure you point out something true or helpful in a response. Don't just move on. Build community with follow-up questions, asking how other students have experienced similar things or how a truth has shaped their understanding of God and the Scripture you're studying.

Keep God's Word Central. Opinions and experiences can be helpful, but God has given us the truth. Trust Scripture to be the authority and God's Spirit to work in students lives. You can't change anyone, but God can. Continually point people to the Word and to active steps of faith.

Keep Connecting. Encourage group members with thoughts, commitments, or questions from the session by connecting through emails, texts, and social media. Build deeper friendships by planning or spontaneously inviting group members to join you outside your regularly scheduled group time for meals; fun activities; and projects around your home, church, or community. The more students are comfortable with one another and involved in one another's lives, the more they'll look forward to being together.

ABOUT THE AUTHOR

At the age of twenty-seven, J.D. Greear became the pastor of a forty-year-old neighborhood church. In the years since, that congregation of four hundred has grown to more than five thousand in weekly attendance. Today, the Summit Church—located in Raleigh-Durham, North Carolina—is one of the fastest-growing churches in North America.

Pastor J.D.'s messages aren't intended just to show people how to live better lives; his goal is to leave people in awe of God's amazing love. Because of his belief in the power of the gospel, pastor J.D. has led the Summit to set a goal of planting more than one thousand gospel-centered churches in the next 40 years.

Pastor J.D. holds a PhD in systematic theology from Southeastern Baptist Theological Seminary. He also lived and worked among Muslims in Southeast Asia for two years and wrote *Breaking the Islam Code*. J.D. and his beautiful wife, Veronica, have four ridiculously cute kids: Kharis, Alethia, Ryah, and Adon.

Unless God calls him elsewhere, pastor J.D. plans to stay at the Summit Church until he preaches his last sermon at his own funeral before saying goodbye and hopping into the casket.

INTRODUCTION

What's the most important priority in your life? What about in your church? These are questions worthy of your time and attention. If you're a follower of Jesus, the answer to both questions should be the same: the gospel of Jesus Christ. The most pressing need, I believe, for followers of Jesus today is the need to elevate the gospel above all.

You see, the gospel is more than simply the entry rite into Christianity, the ABCs, the diving board off which we jump into the pool of Christianity. It's the whole pool.

In 1 Corinthians 2:2 Paul said he had resolved "to know nothing" while he was with the Corinthians "except Jesus Christ and him crucified." In 1 Corinthians 15:3 he said the gospel was "most important."

In Romans Paul said:

> *I am not ashamed of the gospel, because it is the power of God for salvation. ... In it the righteousness of God is revealed from faith to faith.*
> **ROMANS 1:16-17**

Paul went on to explain that only by renewing ourselves in the mercies of God can we discern the perfect and acceptable will of God (see 12:1-2).

Without giving the gospel intentional focus, we'll make programs, politics, preferences, petty differences, or any number of lesser priorities more important. Jesus has called us to more.

The goal of this Bible study is to help you see the unique glory of God revealed through the grace of the gospel. Once that message becomes above all in your life, you'll bear incredible fruit for the kingdom of our Lord.

SESSION 1

GOSPEL
ABOVE
ALL

START

Welcome to group session 1 of Gospel Above All.

What would you say is most important in your life?

How is what's most important to you reflected in your actions? Can you give an example from your life?

What is most important to us will determine our actions because we act in accordance with our desires. We talk about, celebrate, and look forward to the activities, events, and relationships we love. Where does the gospel fit into our list of priorities? Does it come first, or is it something we consider only occasionally? *Gospel Above All* is a call to put the gospel ahead of absolutely everything.

As followers of Jesus, we need to reinforce our identity as a gospel people. We don't find our unity in the sports or activities we engage in, our hobbies, or even the groups of friends we hang out with. Followers of Jesus will fight the temptation to pretend to be someone they are not while at school or on social media, because they know their identity is in Christ who loves them and gave Himself for them. We find our unity in the gospel. Everything else is secondary. Over the next eight weeks, we'll consider together what it means to truly place the gospel above all.

WATCH

Refer to this viewer guide as you watch video session 1.

The gospel is the ___good___ ___news___ that God loves us, that Jesus Christ came to earth to suffer the penalty for our sin and die in our place so that we could be restored to God, reconciled to Him, and live with Him forever.

The gospel is not just the way we ___begin___ in Christ. It's also the way we ___grow___ in Christ.

For the gospel to be above all, it's got to go deep in us to the point that it ___transforms___ us from the inside out and ___changes___ all our affections, mentality, and behavior.

The future of the church in America hinges on whether God's people ___return___ to the gospel as the central, defining element in their lives and the defining focus of their ___mission___.

Take Notes:

The gospel

The first evangelists were messengers who told good news about battles

DISCUSS

Use the following questions to discuss the video teaching.

Read 1 Corinthians 2:2 together.

*I decided to know nothing among you except
Jesus Christ and him crucified.*

1 CORINTHIANS 2:2

Paul believed the gospel was the most important message in the world. Although we might agree with what Paul said, we often deny it with our actions and the attention of our hearts. No other concern should come before our dedication to the gospel. All we are and all we do as followers of Jesus flows from the gospel.

What are some messages or concerns we elevate above the gospel in our churches and in our lives?

Why is the gospel good news to you? Why is it good news to the people in your neighborhood, school, and family?

According to Jesus, the gospel is the sum of Jesus' ministry. In Greek, the word *gospel* literally means good news. The origins of this word extend beyond Christianity. When a Roman general won a military victory, the gospel of that general's victory went forth to alert the different parts of the empire about His success.

In the same way, the gospel of Jesus Christ signals Jesus' victory over sin, death, and the grave. It's the message that though we're desperately broken by sin, Jesus came to earth, lived the life we couldn't live, died the death we deserved to die, and rose again in victory over sin and death. Because of what Jesus did to provide salvation, we can now be resurrected from the dead and reconciled to God. We were created for this kind of relationship with God.

Why do Christians need the gospel just as much as non-Christians?

In the video teaching J. D. said, "The fire to do in the Christian life comes from being soaked in the fuel of what has been done." Growth in the Christian life comes from being rooted in the gospel. The gospel isn't just an entry into the Christian faith but into the entirety of the Christian life.

How does the gospel lead us to deeper trust in and obedience to God? In what ways have you seen this type of growth in your life?

The gospel has far-reaching implications for the way we study God's Word, our message as Christian people, how we think politically, the type of culture we create, and the way we love our neighbors. The rest of this study will deal with all of these topics.

What would you say Christians are known for in your community? How do we become people characterized by the gospel message?

Many of us are probably growing tired of the constant political battles being waged in our culture. The people around us probably are too. The church must allow the gospel to shape our political involvement. The opportunity to create a refuge from the incessant bickering has never been stronger. To do this, we have to make room for differences of opinion on secondary matters, because the gospel is too important to be compromised by political arguments. We must be a people full of grace, just like Jesus.

The gospel reminds us that God loves everyone. Jesus invites all people to be reconciled to God through Him. How should the gospel change the way we see and relate to people who are different than us?

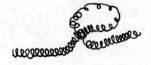

RESPOND

Use these questions to apply today's teaching.

As we close our time together today, let's briefly reflect on a few ideas we've introduced in this session and look forward to the group sessions ahead.

What might it look like when the gospel is above all in our churches? In our student ministry? In our lives?

Examine the table of contents to see the topics we'll cover. Which upcoming session topic are you most looking forward to? Why?

PRAYER

Close the session with prayer.

Father God, in a world full of competing messages and conflicting claims, You've given us the one truth that's above all other truths—the gospel of Jesus Christ. Only one message saves, and we've heard it and believed. From our love for the truth and care for our neighbor, would You allow this message to become a matter of first importance in our lives? Please give us grace to lift up the gospel above all.

Remind group members to complete this week's personal study.

GOSPEL ABOVE ALL

What Is the Gospel?

The word *gospel* has become so common in some circles that it has been stripped of much of its power and meaning. But the word was so central to Jesus' ministry that I simply can't get away from it. So what exactly do we mean when we say "gospel"?

How would you describe the gospel in one word?

What about in one sentence?

Jesus taking the punishment for my sin

The key word in all the gospel is *substitution*. At the church I pastor we say the gospel in four words is "Jesus in my place." Jesus went to the cross, not only to die *for* us but to die *instead* of us. He took our burden of sin so we could put on His righteousness. This is the good news of the gospel: Jesus lived the life we were supposed to live and died the death we were condemned to die. The apostle Paul summarized it this way:

> I passed on to you as most important what I also received: that Christ
> died for our sins according to the Scriptures, that he was buried,
> that he was raised on the third day according to the Scriptures.
>
> **1 CORINTHIANS 15:3-4**

What elements did Paul include in his concise gospel statement? Where do you see "Jesus in my place" in these verses?

Jesus died "for our sins" (v. 3). We're sinful; Jesus is sinless. Jesus died in our place for our sins on the cross. He died as our substitute. The principle of substitution separates Jesus' gospel from every other religion. The great religions of the world all teach that we must do something to please God. *Go here. Say this. Do this. Don't do that. Pray this. Chant that.* If we do these things often enough and well enough, God will accept us—or so we hope.

But the gospel is about what Jesus has done for us. In every other religion, the prophet is a teacher who gives us a plan to earn God's favor. In Christianity, we have the story of a Savior who has earned God's favor on our behalf and gives it to us as a gift. Other religious systems are about what you do; Christianity is about what has been done for you.

In what areas of life do you feel as though you need to "earn your keep"?

School, some friendships

How have you transferred this need to prove yourself to your relationship with God?

Why is the message of the gospel—the truth that in His grace God has done everything necessary for your salvation—a message we need to reflect on every day?

The Gospel Is for Christians Too

We need to ask and answer the previous question because the gospel is for Christians too. Although believers might not deny the gospel, we tend to forget it. For many of us, the gospel functions solely as the entry into Christianity. It's the prayer we pray to begin our relationship with Jesus, the diving board we jump off of into the pool of the real Christian life.

However, the gospel isn't just the diving board into the pool of Christianity; it's the pool itself. It's not only the way we begin in Christ; it's also the way we grow in Christ. All of the Christian life flows from the good news of what Jesus has done.

What are some ways you've minimized or misunderstood the gospel's ongoing importance in your faith?

If you're honest, do you ever feel you've moved beyond the simple gospel message? If so, why?

Paul recognized this tendency when he said the gospel was "most important" (v. 3). He didn't see the gospel as just the doorway into the Christian faith. The gospel is the main priority in the Christian life. It can never be less than primary. Growth in the Christian life isn't about going *beyond* the gospel but rooting ourselves more deeply in the truth of the gospel. The purest waters from the spring of life are found by digging deeper, not wider, into the gospel well.

> **List some markers we commonly use to determine growth in the Christian life. How are those markers tied to a deepening faith in the gospel?**

Our hearts are hardwired to base our worth on our performance or efforts. Grace doesn't come naturally to us. Therefore, we need to remind ourselves of the gospel message often because it remains good news even for those of us who've followed Christ for years.

> **What are some ways you could remind yourself of the gospel daily?**

Our world is sick and needs the healing balm of the gospel. We must avoid the temptation to let any other issues replace the centrality of the gospel in our lives. The need is too great, the hour is too near, and the beauty of the gospel is too precious for us to define ourselves by anything else. The gospel must be above all.

PRAYER AND REFLECTION

Spend some time in silence before the Lord doing two things.
1. Express gratitude for what Jesus has done for you in the gospel.
2. Ask Him to help you identify areas in your life where you're trusting in something other than the gospel of grace or where you've allowed something else to become a matter of first importance.

ENGAGE WITH YOUR COMMUNITY

The purpose of this section is to help you think through key ideas from this week's study with other members of your group. Take some time to thoughtfully consider the following questions, and then record your responses. Reach out to one or two members of your group and discuss your answers together.

The gospel is above all preferences and plans. It's more important than any denominational or doctrinal distinctives. Yet in practice the gospel often gets pushed to the background. This exercise is designed to help you identify what you prize above the gospel.

What priorities do you elevate to a higher level of importance than you should?

School, my personal comfort

Why should the gospel rule over all of these lesser concerns?

It's more important than everything

How can you ensure that the gospel remains most important in your life?

Going to church, reading my Bible, asking God for help, reminding myself constantly

NOT JUST THE DIVING BOARD

Earlier this week, we established that the gospel should be the most important truth in our lives. Today we're going to examine why.

You probably haven't ever had a reason to use a plumb line, but it's a remarkably simple, helpful tool. It's a piece of cord with a weight attached to the end. When the cord is allowed to hang freely, the weight naturally creates a perfectly vertical line. Painters, builders, and other craftsmen use this tool to keep their work level and straight. The plumb line ensures that a proper foundation is being built.

At The Summit—the church I pastor—we have a series of short, catchy statements we use as rallying points, both for our staff and for the entire church. They sum up our ministry philosophy in memorable phrases. They're called plumb lines.

Plumb line 1 at The Summit is:

> *The gospel isn't just the diving board; it's the pool.*

This statement is important to consider, because Christianity teaches something fundamentally different from every other religion. Every other religion says if you change, you'll be accepted. But Christianity says, "Because you've been accepted, therefore change." Christianity doesn't proclaim good advice but good news. And that news transforms us from the inside out.

What other world religions are you familiar with? How is Christianity fundamentally different?

How is Christianity distinct from the cultural messages we encounter every day?

Cultural messages are individualistic — all centered on ourselves and what we can do, not what's been done for us

The gospel of grace is a radically unique, liberating message in a world full of contrary ideas that promise to bring us life and peace but can't deliver on what they promise. Believers have a tendency to forget the gospel and start believing those other messages.

The gospel of grace is also a unique, liberating message in a world full of religious commands and restrictions. It's the only message that can really change us. Religion might be able to force outward conformity—at least for a while. But religion can never transform the heart. To borrow Jesus' metaphor, it cleans the outside of the cup but leaves the inside filthy (Matt. 23:26).

However, believing you've been accepted by grace transforms you in a fundamentally different and more profound way.

How has believing the gospel changed you? The way you talk? The way you interact with friends, classmates, or family members?

What makes the change produced by the gospel distinct from other kinds of changes you've made?

The Gospel Gives You Peace and Security with God

Jesus said, "I will not leave you as orphans; I am coming to you" (John 14:18). A faithful father doesn't leave his kids wondering whether he loves them. When I go away on a trip, I don't say to my kids, "Daddy will be back soon ... or maybe he won't. You'll just have to wait and see whether I come back. Sit around and think about that idea while I'm gone and let it compel you to become better children."

Those words wouldn't produce love and loyalty in my children. They might produce a little fear-based obedience, but it's only a matter of time until fear-based obedience turns into father-loathing rebellion. God doesn't want that for us any more than we want that for our friends or family. He wants us to be at peace with Him, which begins by recognizing His compassion for us. Only experiencing the love of God can truly inspire love for God.

The Gospel Releases Power in Your Life

I am not ashamed of the gospel, because it is the power of God for salvation to everyone who believes, first to the Jew, and also to the Greek.

ROMANS 1:16

The gospel is the power of God. The same power that surged through Jesus' ministry during His time on earth is available to us today. It's the power of the Holy Spirit, and it comes into our lives when we believe the gospel. As Paul expressed it, when we behold the glory of God in the face of Christ, we're "transformed into the same image from glory to glory" (2 Cor. 3:18). Through Jesus, we encounter the only message that's able to save.

> **Reread Romans 1:16. If the gospel is the only message that saves, why would we ever be ashamed of it? What unique power has the gospel given us?**

People who experience the grace and mercy of God in Christ should constantly, loudly, unashamedly talk about the gospel. We have no trouble talking about other things we love. How much more should we talk about the message that has brought us peace with God?

Nothing we do should ever lack a gospel motivation and a gospel focus. Jesus and His gospel are the center of all we do. He's the ultimate hero of Scripture. He's the Lord of our churches. He's the point. He's our chief plumb line. And He alone holds the power.

PRAYER AND REFLECTION

Thank God that your righteousness and standing before Him can't be earned. Ask Him for grace to stop trying to earn favor and to start embracing the love and compassion available to you in Christ. Pray that the Holy Spirit will daily remind you of what Christ has done for You and will help you make that message the center of your life.

ENGAGE WITH THE WORLD

The purpose of this section is to help you process key ideas from this week's study and think differently about the way you engage with the world. Take some time to thoughtfully consider the following questions. Then record your responses.

What's most important to us informs the way we interact with the world. Jesus taught that what comes out of us begins in our hearts (Matt. 15:10-20). For example, if our chief motivation in life is to achieve success, to be a good friend, or to be a moral person, those heart desires will guide the way we live. Because we're gospel people, the motivation at the center of who we are should be the gospel of Jesus Christ.

What's your primary motivation? Is it the gospel or something else? If it's not the gospel, what do you need to let go of to allow the gospel to bear fruit? Use this chart to record your thoughts.

Motivation	How You Live	Change

Whom do you know who models gospel motivation well? What could you learn from the work God is doing in his or her life? Take time to connect with that person this week and learn from his or her example.

SESSION 2

GOSPEL
CHANGE

START

Welcome to group session 2 of Gospel Above All.

As you completed the personal study last week, what was one key point that stood out to you?

Last week we looked at what the gospel is and why that message is more essential than any other message. This week we'll get more practical.

Do you believe the gospel applies to the little details of our lives? Why or why not?

The gospel isn't an abstract truth we reflect on without ever acting. The gospel changes everything about the way we live. Once we've believed the gospel, the natural question to ask next is: "What am I supposed to do with this message?" This week we'll consider ways the gospel applies to our day-to-day lives.

WATCH

Refer to this viewer guide as you watch video session 2.

Every day is an opportunity to be ___transformed___ increasingly into the ___image___ of Christ.

The only way I can truly understand the ___beauty___ of who I am in Christ is to behold ___Christ___.

Seeing who God is helps you ___understand___ who you are, and knowing who you are tells you there are ___implications___ for the way you live your life.

We're exercising a joyful obedience out of ___gratitude___. It's not a grudging obedience out of ___fear___.

Just as you're asking the Holy Spirit to turn your eyes toward ___God___, you're also asking Him to turn your eyes toward ___others___.

We cannot love ourselves rightly until we understand our relationship to ___God___.

Grace is not opposed to ___effort___. It's only opposed to ___earning___.

Take Notes:

It's important to remind ourselves about the Gospel daily, so the Bible is less like a to-do list and more like good news

It's more comfortable to compare ourselves to "lesser" people, but it's better to compare ourselves to God
To be in his image, we have to know his image.

DISCUSS

Use the following questions to discuss the video teaching.

Have you ever heard the advice that you should preach the gospel to yourself daily? What does that mean?

What's wrong with preaching the gospel to others but not to ourselves?

On the video, Jen said preaching the gospel to yourself means taking the message of grace and applying it to your daily life. One reason we fail to apply the gospel to many areas of our lives is that we approach the Bible the wrong way.

Many of us have been taught that the Bible is a guide book for life. Although the Bible contains abundant direction for our lives; that's not the primary reason it exists. The main point of the Bible isn't how to live but how to know God. We come to know God by the gospel, the central message of the Bible.

What happens to our spiritual lives when we reduce the Bible to a guidebook for life instead of a means to know God?

The first of Martin Luther's *Ninety-Five Theses* says, "When our Lord and Master Jesus Christ said, 'Repent' (Matt. 4:17), he willed the entire life of believers to be one of repentance." When we encounter a transcendent vision of God, we should walk away worshiping. Coming face-to-face with the One who's perfectly holy and good should lead us to repent and receive forgiveness and grace. Realizing how unlike God we are should move us to repent.

Why should people who've believed the gospel regularly repent? Why might continual repentance be an unpopular idea today?

Repentance is an unpopular notion today because it means something essential to our nature needs to be corrected. Such a question strikes at the heart of a world that's asking, "Who am I?" One idea J. D. and Jen discussed on the video was this: Who God is, as defined by Scripture, should shape how we live.

A better question than "Who am I?" is "Who is Jesus?" Then we should ask, "How should we live in light of who He is?" We can't know who we are until we understand who God is.

Read 1 John 4:19. Why does knowing that God loved us lead us to love Him and feel accepted by Him?

As J. D. said in video session 1, "The fire to do in the Christian life comes from being soaked in the fuel of what has been done." What has been done for us in the gospel frees us to obey God's commands because we're no longer motivated by obligation but by the joy of being known, loved, and accepted by God. Gospel change empowers grace-driven effort toward obedience.

What is it about us that causes us to seek approval through rule following? How is grace-driven effort entirely different from rule following?

J. D. and Jen both expressed their personal struggles as rule followers. This struggle likely resonated with many of you. God isn't seeking just obedience; He's seeking a whole new kind of obedience. Gospel-motivated obedience grows from desire. We pursue righteous works because we crave righteousness. This craving comes from the sanctifying work of the Holy Spirit in our lives.

Read Romans 8:14-16. How does the Holy Spirit help us understand we're loved by God? How does this knowledge help us live out the gospel in our daily lives?

RESPOND

Use these questions to apply today's teaching.

I hope this session has helped you see that gospel change happens as we behold the face of Jesus, receive approval from Him, and live with Spirit-enabled intentionality and effort. By God's grace, the way these truths are incorporated into our lives is through continual contact with God in His Word. Reading the Bible shouldn't be a burden or a chore. Instead, it should be a means for us to see and know God better.

> **Why is consistent Bible reading essential for gospel change?**

> **Do you have a plan to spend dedicated time in the Scriptures each week? If not, who might be able to help you read the Bible?**

PRAYER

Close the session with prayer.

We thank You, God, that today isn't another day when we have to try and earn anything from You. Instead, it is a day when we can ask the Spirit to work through us so all godliness may be manifested and others might look at us and see the image of Christ.

Remind group members to complete this week's personal study.

1. Martin Luther, "The Ninety-Five Theses," accessed November 6, 2018, https://www.luther.de/en/95thesen.html.

DIAGNOSIS VERSUS PRESCRIPTION

In this week's group session we talked about what it means for the gospel to take root and bear fruit in our hearts and lives. In today's personal study we will examine one reason we have trouble living out the gospel and one tool to help us regularly meditate on the gospel.

Rate yourself: Is regular reflection on the gospel part of your life?

|||||||||||||||||||||||||||||||||||||||||||||||||||||||||||||||||||||

Not a part of my life   **Regular rhythm**

Diagnosis

One absolutely critical factor in interpreting the Bible is recognizing the difference between diagnosis and prescription. Diagnosis describes what's wrong in our lives; prescription tells us what to do about it.

Many passages in the Bible tell us that if certain traits or actions aren't true of us, we're not saved. For example, if we aren't generous to the poor (Jas. 2:15-17), filled with love for the church (1 John 4:21), concerned about and working on behalf of the persecuted church (Matt. 25:40-41), and fighting sin in our lives (1 John 3:8-10), we're not saved. A heart that has been changed by God will respond differently to these issues.

However, we can go majorly wrong when we turn *diagnosis* into the *prescription*. How do we fix our hearts if we love sin, aren't generous, or care more about ourselves than people in need?

When have you tried to fix your sin on your own? What were the results?

In John 6:28 the crowd that had been following Jesus asked, "What can we do to perform the works of God?" The fact that they asked the question in the first place shows that they misunderstood something about Jesus. His answer showed that they didn't know what the works of God were. Jesus responded, "This is the work of God—that you believe in the one he has sent" (John 6:29). That's our work as followers of Christ.

God's work isn't seeking justice, going on mission, advocating for the poor, memorizing Scripture, committing to biblical community, or any other behavior. It's the simple act of believing in Jesus. When we've done that, we'll naturally be concerned about the poor, love Scripture, and build up the church. Those actions are the fruit of faith in the gospel.

Why do you imagine it's so easy for us to confuse serving the Lord with faith in the Lord?

When do you find you're most tempted to work for your faith?

Obedience to God's commands is the natural result of truly believing the gospel. Lovelessness is a diagnosis of spiritual death. The prescription for lovelessness isn't to become more loving. Even a radical commitment to love will diminish over time, leaving you exhausted and disappointed in your inability to love as strongly as you wish you could. Faith in the gospel is the only quality that makes us alive. The Holy Spirit at work in our hearts is the only One who can produce a love that won't run out. That's why true followers of Jesus should always spend more time worshiping in the presence of God than commanding other people to perform works for Him.

Diagnose your inner life. Are you unloving? Oblivious to the suffering around you? Dishonest? All of the above? What would be a gospel-centered answer to the current state of your heart?

Prescription

Although the only way to see progress in the Christian life is a deepening trust in the gospel, certain practices can anchor our hearts in the simple truths of the gospel.

Every day I pray the following prayer to fortify my mind in the gospel. I call it the gospel prayer. This isn't a magical prayer, and I didn't create the ideas. It came about a few years ago as I began to recognize the centrality of the gospel to all of Scripture and all of the Christian life. This prayer has become my way of applying the gospel to my daily life.

Because I'm in Christ ...

1. *There's nothing I can do that would make You love me more, and there's nothing I've done that would make You love me less.*

2. *Your presence and approval are all I need for everlasting joy.*

3. *As You've been to me, so I'll be to others.*

4. *As I pray, I'll measure Your compassion by the cross and Your power by the resurrection.*

Take a few moments to consider and pray each statement in the gospel prayer. Which statement resonates with you the most?

How could you benefit from regularly praying this prayer or one like it?

PRAYER AND REFLECTION

Identify ways you've been trying to earn God's favor, release them to God, and receive the grace that comes with the gospel. Take time to pray the gospel prayer again, slowly embracing the simple truth that God loves you, died for you, and deeply cares you.

ENGAGE WITH YOUR COMMUNITY

The purpose of this section is to help you process key ideas from this week's study with other members of your group. Take some time to thoughtfully consider the following questions. Then record your responses. Reach out to one or two members of your group and discuss your answers. Today you'll focus on a spiritual discipline that helps you press the gospel deeper into your heart: memorizing Scripture.

Have you ever memorized Scripture before?
What practical difference did it make in your life?

Below is a well-known passage of Scripture from Paul's letter to the Galatians.

The fruit of the Spirit is love, joy, peace, patience, kindness, goodness, faithfulness, gentleness, and self-control. The law is not against such things. Now those who belong to Christ Jesus have crucified the flesh with its passions and desires. If we live by the Spirit, let us also keep in step with the Spirit.

GALATIANS 5:22-25

The words of Scripture are breathed out by God. When we take these words and push them into our souls, we create a reservoir of truth we can pull from when we wish to stop and drink from the well of God's truth.

The fruit of the Spirit consists of godly character traits all Christians possess because the Spirit of Christ lives in them. We don't work to cultivate these qualities; they're born in us when we trust in Christ and walk in the Holy Spirit.

Memorization tips. Read each verse in the passage aloud ten times. Then look away and repeat the verse ten times from memory. When you've memorized one verse, move on to the next one. Try memorizing one verse a day. Reach out to someone in the group for accountability in memorization. Ask how it's going and share what you're learning.

FRUIT PRODUCED BY THE GOSPEL

Thinking about the fruit of the Spirit, we encounter a common problem. Typically, we look a this list and try to make ourselves be more loving, joyful, peaceful, patient, good, or self-controlled by sheer force of will. Gospel growth doesn't happen that way. There's a better approach to spiritual growth than trying to grow by our own strength. Today we'll consider further thoughts on Galatians 5:22-25 and gospel change.

Healthy Fruit Comes from Deep Roots

With a literal plant you don't grow fruit by focusing on the fruit. Fruit happens when the roots are deep and healthy. The same is true in our spiritual lives.

Some Christians approach spiritual growth like stapling roses to a dead rosebush. If you drive by and look at the rosebush, you might think it's healthy. But stapling roses onto a stalk doesn't produce life. In the same way, you won't grow spiritually by trying to add love, joy, peace, and the other characteristics to your life. You can grow only by driving your roots deep into Christ. The more you embrace His love and promise in the gospel, the more spiritual fruit will naturally appear in your life.

As you read the fruit of the Spirit, you may think: *Yikes! I'm so bad. I have no love, joy, peace, patience, kindness, or goodness. And I definitely have no self-control. Maybe this week I can work on kindness and patience.*

But instead of looking at yourself, you need to look at Jesus and believe that in Christ you are righteous. In Him, you are chosen before the foundation of the world and so precious to Him that Jesus poured out His blood for you. You are not a slave but a son or a daughter, blessed with every spiritual blessing in the heavenly places. You are filled with all the fullness of God and set apart by God for good works that you should go and walk in them.

What changes about your outlook when you consider who you are instead of what you lack? Which do you do more often?

For every look you take at yourself, grieving your fruitlessness (a great start), take ten looks at Christ, bragging about His faithfulness.

Your Most Immature Fruit

When you read Galatians 5, you might wonder about Paul's grammar in verse 22. Paul said, "The fruit of the Spirit is ..." (singular) and then provided a plural list. Shouldn't he have said, "The fruits of the Spirit are ..."? Paul wasn't being a sloppy grammarian. He was pointing out that these aren't separate virtues you staple onto your life but the collective evidence of Christ in you. If you are united to Christ by faith, then all the fruits of the Spirit will begin showing up in your heart and consequently in your daily life.

Sometimes we confuse personality traits for spiritual fruit. For example, some Christians are more stoic by nature, so we look at them and say, "That person has patience." But they're not joyful or kind. Or a Christian who's gentle and kind to others may never tell people about Jesus. When you find one virtue that's far out of balance with the others, it's likely you're looking not at gospel fruit but at personality traits.

Where Jesus is, all the fruit grows as one. You're bold and kind, gentle and compassionate, patient and joyful. Therefore, you're only as mature as your most immature fruit. When you observe an area where you're fruitless, this is where you haven't yet believed and applied the gospel to your life.

> **In what areas do you need to believe and apply the gospel for growth?**

Walk by the Spirit

I say then, walk by the Spirit and you will certainly not carry out the desire of the flesh.
GALATIANS 5:16

Notice the order in Galatians 5:16. "Walk by the Spirit." Then "you will certainly not carry out the desire of the flesh." Most people tend to reverse the order. We think we have to avoid sin in order to be filled with the Spirit. But Paul said walking by the Spirit comes first, because without the Spirit you'll never be able to say no to the lusts of the flesh.

What about you? Do you try and kill sin before you walk by the Spirit? What makes this strategy seem as if it would work for us?

The Greek word for *desire* in verse 16 means "inordinate craving," or the feeling that you need something to be alive. This idea goes all the way back to what happened in the garden of Eden. When Adam and Eve first sinned, they were stripped of God's acceptance, so their souls felt naked, and naked souls look for clothing. This is a picture of the way we live our lives. Feeling vulnerable and spiritually naked, we look for something to replace what God used to be to us.

Sin has created a God-shaped void in our lives that we try to fill with many other things. But the only way to escape these cravings is by being reunited with God and walking by the Spirit. Until we begin walking by the Spirit, our attempts to control the flesh won't work because our desires are too strong.

What are the people around you trying to fill their God-shaped void with? What fruit do you observe in their lives?

What are some common answers you see our culture giving to our problem with sin?

The Holy Spirit's power is released in us by believing this truth daily: "It is finished" (John 19:30). The first time we believed "it is finished," we were released from the penalty of sin. As we continue to believe it, the Spirit releases us from the power of sin.

PRAYER AND REFLECTION

Pray that you'll walk by the Spirit daily. Ask for His power and presence as you seek to deny the desires of your flesh.

ENGAGE WITH THE WORLD

The purpose of this section is to help you process key ideas from this week's study and think differently about the way you engage with the world. Take some time to thoughtfully consider the following questions. Then record your responses.

We saw that all people have a God-sized void caused by sin, and we identified ways the people we know are trying to fill that void. Part of what it means to be changed by the gospel is to want to see others changed by the gospel. At some point this week, have a conversation with a lost person you know and listen to them. Try to identify the way they're finding their identity. Listen and discern what they must believe about God to find their identity this way. Look for ways to share with them the way you find your identity.

Who were you able to talk to?

Where were they finding their identity?
Would you say they're happy or fulfilled?

Were you able to share with them the source
of your identity? If so, how did that go?

When will you make time to see them again?

GOSPEL
MISSION

START

Welcome to group session 3 of Gospel Above All.

> **Last week's personal study asked you to memorize Galatians 5:22-25. How did that go? What did you learn?**

> **How did you first come to know Jesus? Who has helped you grow in your faith?**

Last week, we looked at the gospel's impact on our personal lives. This week we'll look at what happens when we share with others God's transforming work in us.

God uses ordinary people to carry out His mission of multiplying disciples. To be a follower of Jesus is to be a disciple who multiplies the gospel. We have no greater mission.

WATCH

Refer to this viewer guide as you watch video session 3.

God has created us, crafted us, saved us, blessed us ultimately for the spread of _____ _____ in the world.

Every Christian is supposed to be on mission where we _____ and then be open to going wherever God might _____.

The question is no longer _____ you're called. The question is _____ and _____.

Every follower of Christ has the Spirit of God _____ in them for the purpose of the _____ of the gospel through them.

We're a fellowship of disciple _____, not an audience of _____.

Don't underestimate how your disciple making right where you _____ is a part of a grand plan to get the gospel to the _____ of the earth.

Over _____ _____ people groups have little to no access to the gospel.

Every saved person this side of _____ owes the gospel to every unsaved person this side of _____.

Take Notes:

ANSWERS: His glory / live, lead / if, where, how / dwelling, spread / makers, spectators / live, ends / six thousand / heaven, hell

DISCUSS

Use the following questions to discuss the video teaching.

The gospel is the central message of the Bible, and gospel mission is a central feature of that message. From cover to cover, the Bible tells the story of the God who created, crafted, saved, and blessed us for the spread of His glory in the world. Because the gospel is true, the story must be told.

> **In the video, David Platt described missions as "the spread of the glory of God in the world." How does this definition challenge your understanding of what it means to live on mission?**

We tend to think of missions only as traveling cross-culturally to meet physical needs and share the gospel. Missions is actually much broader. Each of us glorifies God in the unique place where God has called us in life. In that sense, we're all on mission.

Though we're all called to be on mission, God has also called uniquely gifted Christians to take the gospel to places that have little or no access to the gospel. The common element in both callings is the desire for God to be glorified in all the earth.

> **Pastor J. D. mentioned that in John 16:7 Jesus taught that it was good for Him to leave. Why was Jesus' ascension to heaven better for our mission?**

Because we all have the same Spirit and the same Word Jesus had, none of us are exempt from participating in His mission. Every disciple is called to be a disciple maker.

> **Read Matthew 28:18-20. How would you define what it means to make a disciple? What components of disciple making did Jesus identify?**

The Great Commission centers on one central command: "Make disciples" (v. 19). Disciples are created when we go into the world and share the gospel. Discipleship continues as people are baptized, join the church, and are taught to obey all Jesus commanded. We tend to think about discipleship, like missions, as a church program. Yet, like I pointed out in the video, 75 percent of discipleship occurs informally.

What opportunities do you have to show someone what it means to follow Christ? How have you learned to follow Jesus?

Jesus changed the entire world by spending three years investing His life in twelve men in a relatively small location. That was His entire plan. Yes, it involved intentional teaching, but much of Jesus' method of discipleship involved showing the disciples what it means to follow God by simply living His life with them. Jesus' plan for taking the gospel to the nations is disciple making.

Read Romans 1:14-16. How did Paul describe His urgency to share the gospel?

David Platt mentioned several times in the video that Christians need to live with an open hand. What would change about your life if you allowed God to fully determine the course of your life?

Paul was obligated to take the gospel to people who hadn't heard. He was eager to preach, and he was unashamed. Every believer is responsible to submit to God's lead and go wherever He wills. We all have a calling to make disciples and the capacity to carry out that calling. The question is: What will you do with it?

RESPOND

Use these questions to apply today's teaching.

In the video, David Platt identified three places each of us can begin making disciples: at home, at work, and at play. What opportunities exist for you to make disciples in these three areas?

God loves the people around you so much that He has placed you in their lives with a supernatural power to share the gospel. Many of us will be called to make disciples where we are. Yet with billions of people in the world with no access to the gospel, many of us will be called to go to them as well.

David shared stories about people in his church who are living with an open hand and allowing God to use them. The beauty of making disciples is that we can participate in a process that will extend far beyond us. Committing ourselves to spread God's glory allows us to take part in a plan with eternal significance. Stop and consider how you'll respond to God's call.

Is there an area of the world you feel a burden to pray for, give money for gospel work there, or visit on a short-term mission trip?

PRAYER

Close the session with prayer.

As you end your time together, pray for the responses people gave in the previous section. Ask God to use your group to make His glory known in all the earth.

Remind group members to complete this week's personal study.

WITHOUT THIS, NOTHING ELSE MATTERS

What would you say is the one pursuit to which all followers of Jesus should give their time? Why?

spreading the gospel

How do you think other Christians you know would answer this question?

Many skills contribute to effective ministry, but there's one without which everything else we do is useless. That one skill is making disciples. If we busy ourselves with any other activities—even good ones—but neglect this crucial aspect of our calling, we'll be unsuccessful in our mission. Without this one thing, we'll fail.

For a disciple, all of life should be focused on disciple making. The only direct command in the Great Commission (Matt. 28:19-20) is to make disciples. Making disciples is the central organizing principle of the church. In his book *The Master Plan of Evangelism* Robert Coleman wrote:

> The Great Commission is not merely to go to the ends of the earth preaching the gospel (Mark 16:15), nor to baptize a lot of converts into the name of the triune God, nor to teach them the precepts of Christ, but to "make disciples"—to build people like themselves who were so constrained by the commission of Christ that they not only followed his way but led others to as well.[1]

Have you ever been in a church culture in which multiplying disciples was the chief concern? What was that like?

Why is it so easy for believers to pursue lesser things instead of making disciples?

It's easier

Multiplication Begins with Discipleship

The church was designed to grow through the multiplication of disciples, yet many churches grow through what might be called transfer growth. Maybe you've heard of a church experiencing explosive growth and revival as the result of a shift in strategy or programming. But how many conversions and baptisms take place? Much of what we count as church growth actually comes from members transferring from a church that doesn't suit their preferences to one that does. A church can grow, even explosively, without one person trusting Christ as Savior and Lord. This pattern of growth isn't what Jesus had in mind in the Great Commission.

I've been inspired watching our college ministry because it makes disciples extremely well. Each year it launches about fifty students into ministry, most of whom come from non-Christian backgrounds. A couple of years ago it sent a full-time church-planting team to Southeast Asia that consisted of eight college graduates, seven of whom had become Christians at our church during college. The next year the college ministry supplied us with fourteen interns to help reach more students in the area, all of whom had become Christians during their time in college.

The difference? This college ministry puts extraordinary emphasis on discipleship.

To reach more people, we don't need better programs or events; we need better discipleship. Bigger audiences don't equate with more decisions for Christ. If we're going to move the gospel-mission needle, we have to turn unbelievers into church leaders, atheists into missionaries. We have to become good at making disciples.

How have you been discipled in the faith?

If someone asked you to explain how to make a disciple, what would you say?

Easier Than You Think

The prospect of making a disciple may seem daunting. It's natural to feel inadequate. The good news is that making disciples is much less complicated than we make it. All you have to do is teach people what God is teaching you. The key ingredient is intentionality. You show others how to read the Bible. You teach them what it means to pray, give, serve, and worship. Some of this process happens through teaching, but much more happens naturally.

I asked one of the most effective disciplers I know to share his discipleship system. I was expecting a fancy curriculum with a silver-bullet technique. Instead, he sent me a scanned list of verse references he typed by hand on a word processor in the 1980s. He gives this list to people he's trying to bring to faith and asks them to read the verses and write what they think each verse means and what God is saying to them through it. He then meets with them the next week to discuss their answers. After that, he asks them if they want to read a book of Bible together. That was it. No secret sauce, no electrifying jolt of discipleship genius, just simple faith applied to a simple process.

With whom could you walk through a process similar to the one described?

What intimidates you about making disciples? What exhilarates you?

We can't afford to live our Christian lives without ever attending to the one task Jesus gave us. God's will for your life is to make disciples. To miss that purpose is to miss out on the mission.

PRAYER AND REFLECTION

Ask God to place in your path a specific person for you to disciple. Pray for confidence to accept the opportunity God lays in front of you

---

1. Robert Coleman, *The Master Plan of Evangelism,* 2nd ed. (Grand Rapids, MI: Revell, 1993), 104.

ENGAGE WITH YOUR COMMUNITY

The purpose of this section is to help you process key ideas from this week's study with other members of your group. Take some time to thoughtfully consider the following questions. Then record your responses. Reach out to one or two members of your group and discuss your answers together.

Discipleship is a repeatable process. Near the end of Paul's life, he wrote two letters to a young pastor named Timothy. Paul had invested in Timothy and now Paul used the few precious moments he had left on earth to impart wisdom and encouragement to his young friend. Paul wrote:

You, therefore, my son, be strong in the grace that is in Christ Jesus. What you have heard from me in the presence of many witnesses, commit to faithful men who will be able to teach others also.

2 TIMOTHY 2:1-2

Paul took what he knew and taught it to Timothy with the expectation that Timothy would do the same, creating a chain of discipleship. All disciples should have another disciple they're imparting their lives to—a Timothy—and a disciple who's investing in them—a Paul. You may not have a Timothy or a Paul in your life yet and that's OK, but now is the time to start looking.

Who is (or could be) your Paul? Whose walk with Christ is worth imitating? If this process isn't a part of your life yet, whom might you consider asking to disciple you?

Who could be your Timothy? Someone you could guide, pray with, and encourage? What skills or abilities you could use to begin multiplying disciples?

Pray that God will place people in your path to disciple.

MULTIPLICATION, NOT ADDITION

Do you honestly see the Great Commission as the responsibility of every Christian? Why or why not?

Do you think much of the growth of the church happens through uniquely called people or ordinary, faithful Christians? Explain.

Jesus' vision of the church wasn't a group of people gathered around one anointed leader but multiple leaders going into the world in the power of the Holy Spirit. It's a claim that very few of us take seriously. Jesus literally said a multiplicity of Spirit-filled leaders would be greater than His earthly, bodily presence (John 14:12).

Can you imagine the power of a church in which ordinary members know what it means to be filled and led by the Spirit of God? God's plan to glorify Himself in the church never consisted of megachurch pastors with big platforms, cutting-edge art, or expensive buildings. There's nothing wrong with those methods in themselves, but the real power in the church is found the Holy Spirit moving through ordinary people as they carry His presence into the streets.

When have you seen ordinary people contribute to a unique work of God?

Luke, the author of the Book of Acts, went out of his way to show that the biggest advances of the gospel happen through ordinary people. Of all the miracles in Acts, 39 of 40 were done outside the church. We need to expect that kind of ratio today too. In our post-Christian age, fewer and fewer people casually make their way into churches. Many view Christianity the way you or I might view Islam. I wouldn't meander my way into a mosque, even if the music was awesome or the imam was an engaging speaker presenting a helpful series on relationships. Neither can we expect cutting-edge music and entertaining speakers to bring people into the church. People in our day will increasingly have to be reached outside the walls of the church. That means individual believers who are filled with the Spirit are more important than ever.

It also means, as a church, we've got to focus on empowering and equipping our church members for ministry. I'm always encouraged to see our attendance numbers grow, but I know incremental growth won't make a difference for 99 percent of the people we minister to. We need to empower our people to multiply God's power where they already are. As Paul wrote:

> *He himself gave some to be apostles, some prophets, some*
> *evangelists, some pastors and teachers, equipping the saints*
> *for the work of ministry, to build up the body of Christ*
> **EPHESIANS 4:11-12**

When I became a pastor, I left the ministry. My role as a pastor isn't just to carry out ministry but to equip believers to understand their callings in God's mission and to carry them out.

How does Ephesians 4:11-12 challenge your assumptions about the role of pastors in the work of ministry?

Do you tend to think of discipleship primarily as something pastors do? What's wrong with such thinking?

What would change about the church if every Christian took seriously his or her calling to be a disciple who makes disciples?

Ordinary Followers, Extraordinary Calling

When ordinary Christians embrace this idea of calling, the gospel spreads like wildfire. The first time the gospel left Jerusalem, it wasn't in the mouths of the apostles. Regular people "went on their way preaching the word" (Acts 8:4), while the apostles stayed in Jerusalem (v. 1). The first time the gospel actually went out into the world, not a single apostle was involved.

Later in that chapter, Philip (another layman) took the first international mission trip. The Holy Spirit carried him to a desert road where he met an Ethiopian government official, whom Philip led to Christ (vv. 26-38).

The church in Antioch, which served as the hub of missionary activity for the last half of the Book of Acts, wasn't planted by an apostle but simply by some believers whose names Luke didn't even bother to record, presumably because no one would have known whom he was talking about (Acts 11:19-21).

Apollos, a layman, first carried the gospel into Ephesus, and unnamed brothers first established the church in Rome. These Christians didn't travel to Rome on a formal mission trip but were carried there through the normal relocations that come with business and life. As they went, they made disciples in every place (Acts 8:4-8; 18:24–19:1; 28:14-15).

In light of today's study, how would you define your calling?

To be a disciple and make more disciples

How can you use the gifts, talents, and resources God has given you to multiply disciples?

PRAYER AND REFLECTION

Spend a few minutes asking God to help you identify someone you can disciple. As you reflect on disciple making in your life, ask God to stir you out of complacency and lead you into the work He has prepared you to carry out.

ENGAGE WITH THE WORLD

The purpose of this section is to help you process key ideas from this week's study and think differently about the way you engage with the world. Take some time to thoughtfully consider the following questions. Then record your responses.

This week we're discussing the importance of gospel multiplication. Use these questions to evaluate multiplication in your own life.

Rate yourself as a disciple maker. Are you apathetic or eager?

| | | | | | | | | | | | | | | | | | | | | | | | | | | | | | | | | | | | | | | | | | | | | | | | | | | | | | | | | | | |

Apathetic   Eager

How did you become a Christian? Did another believer disciple and invest in you? What might it look like to walk through that same process with another believer?

Consider the approach to making disciples in this week's first personal study, "Without This, Nothing Else Matters." Outline what a disciple-making plan might look like for you.

What avenues exist for you to multiply disciples?

School

Pray that God will place people in your path to disciple.

GOSPEL
EVANGELISM

START

Welcome to group session 4 of Gospel Above All.

Last week we talked about disciple making. Who has recently had a positive impact on your faith?

Discipleship occurs when people take the Spirit of God's work in them and pass it along to another follower of Jesus. God is faithful to take small moments and conversations and use them to multiply His glory on the earth. However, for disciples to be made, people first have to hear the gospel.

The problem is that we haven't made evangelism the central concern of our lives. This week we'll examine evangelism as a way of life, and we'll consider ways we can use our homes as the starting point for Great Commission ministry.

Do you think evangelism is something all Christians should do or only certain Christians who are gifted in evangelism? Explain.

WATCH

Refer to this viewer guide as you watch video session 4.

When I heard we should share our faith, I thought, *Well, I got to get out and do that.*

The ___Cure___ you've discovered is ___greater___ than your personal hang-ups, so you need to overcome that.

Practical Tips for Evangelism

1. Ask, "Who's your __one__?"

2. Have an __unbeliever__ in your home one time a month.

3. Don't sit with someone for more than fifteen minutes before beginning a __conversation__.

4. Pray for __wisdom__.

5. Look for __opportunities__.

6. In a __conversation__ say something related to your faith.

7. Don't cut an __unbeliever__ off and start __disagreeing__ with them.

8. Ask a person, "How can I __pray__ for you?"

9. Use your personal __testimony__.

God is the One who __converts__ people. Our responsibility is to __share__ the gospel.

The gospel isn't about a kind of heavy-handed __moralism__ but rather a __broken__ heart.

It was __unimaginable__ to think that someone like me could be a Christian.

DISCUSS

Use the following questions to discuss the video teaching.

All followers of Jesus, whether they've been walking with Jesus for one day of fifty years, have been given the Great Commission. The call to share our faith is universal, yet we recognize that not all Christians share the gospel. Even Greg Laurie, an evangelist who speaks to crowds of tens of thousands of people, said he's much more comfortable behind the scenes. The goal of this week's study is to give you some practical tips for carrying out Jesus' command to go and make disciples.

> **Read Matthew 13:44. Why should the gospel compel us to do whatever possible to bring someone to Jesus? What lines of comfort do you have trouble crossing to share the gospel?**

The gospel is the most valuable message in the world. The joy we've found in Jesus is worth sharing. We have no resistance to talking about topics that are much less important. Like the man who found a treasure in a field, no comfort is worth keeping if it means keeping Jesus to ourselves. Every Christian can take part in evangelism.

> **Read 1 Corinthians 3:6. In the video, Greg Laurie mentioned that God is the only One who can save people. What's our responsibility? Why is this realization freeing?**

> **J. D. and Greg shared several practical tips for sharing the gospel. Which one would be most helpful for you? Why?**

Sharing our faith isn't complicated. One reason we over-complicate it is that we put too much pressure on ourselves. Our fear of being unsuccessful stops us from sharing. The reality is that we can't save anyone; only God can. All God wants from us is faithfulness. Release yourself from the pressure and embrace the freedom to share. Begin by putting some of J.D.'s and Greg's ideas into practice.

> **Do you know someone in whom God seems to be working? What questions could you ask to engage with him or her?**

Sometimes evangelism looks like a step-by-step formal gospel presentation; often evangelism happens through our relationships. In the video, Rosaria

Butterfield said walking through the door of a Christian's house literally changed her life.

What about the pastor's letter made Rosaria accept his invitation? What can we learn from his example?

Rosaria said she had never understood that the gospel isn't primarily about heavy-handed moralism but about grace saving a broken heart. She didn't learn that from preaching; she learned it from getting to know a Christian. Opening our lives to unbelievers gives credibility to our message. Rosaria never believed someone like her could become a Christian until she became one herself.

What kind of attitude does the relationship-based approach to evangelism take? What are some practical ways you could show kindness or hospitality to someone who doesn't know Jesus?

People are seldom converted at once. It often takes multiple conversations over coffee or around the table before a person receives the gospel. We need to be as patient with our lost friends as Jesus was and is with us. Evangelism through relationships takes time and presents the possibility that we'll get hurt, but bringing someone to Jesus are the most significant connections we can make.

On the video Greg and Rosaria both expressed that their desire for evangelism comes from their own experiences. Both shared personal stories of coming to know Jesus. How could God use your story to help lead someone into the Kingdom?

RESPOND

Use these questions to apply today's teaching.

Of all the practical help the video offered for sharing the gospel, which piece of advice do you plan to put into practice this week?

PRAYER

Close the session with prayer.

As you wrap up, go around the group and ask whether people would be willing to identify and share their "one"— an unbelieving friend they're praying will come to know the Lord. Pray for those people by name and ask God for opportunities to share the gospel.

Remind group members to complete this week's personal study.

YOUR ROLE IN THE MISSION OF GOD

I once saw a fascinating statistic. High-school students (not Christian students) were given a list of possible goals and were asked which three were the most important to them.

Surprisingly, only 18 percent listed "achieving fame or public recognition," and only 25 percent said "working in a high-paying job." So what scored high on the list? Among others, making a difference in the world (96 percent), having one marriage partner for life (82 percent), and having a clear purpose for living (77 percent).[1]

I think most people, regardless of their age, want to know what their divine purpose is—and that they're fulfilling it. In his letter to the Romans, the apostle Paul explained he had found that purpose. Although his calling may not be identical to yours, he laid out the path for discovering yours:

> *I would not dare say anything except what Christ has accomplished*
> *through me by word and deed for the obedience of the Gentiles,*
> *by the power of miraculous signs and wonders, and by the power*
> *of God's Spirit. As a result, I have fully proclaimed the gospel of*
> *Christ from Jerusalem all the way around to Illyricum. My aim is*
> *to preach the gospel where Christ has not been named, so that*
> *I will not build on someone else's foundation, but, as it is written,*
> *Those who were not told about him will see,*
> *and those who have not heard will understand.*
> **ROMANS 15:18-21**

What did Paul identify as His primary ambition in life? What drove him to devote His life to disciple making and evangelism?

By this point in his life, Paul had narrowed down his life to a specific ministry focus: to personally take the gospel where people had never heard it. But how did he arrive at that conclusion? Paul's understanding of his purpose came from two sources, a two-part path of discovery we all must travel.

Understand the Purpose of God in the World

Notice Paul grounded his understanding of his purpose in what Scripture declared to be God's purpose in the world:

> *As it is written,*
> *Those who were not told about him will see,*
> *and those who have not heard will understand.*
> **ROMANS 15:21**

I would have expected Paul to start his explanation of his purpose with the Damascus Road experience. After all, that's where Jesus had told him, "Paul, preaching to the Gentiles is I what I want you to do." If the resurrected Jesus had shown up and literally talked to me, I would have probably led with that. But that's not what Paul did. He started with Scripture. God's purposes in Scripture are the foundation for Paul's purpose in life.

Many people are trying to figure out God's will for their lives, but they haven't stopped to ask what God's purpose is in the world. When I ask people what they want to do, I get answers like "I want to be a doctor," "I want to be an artist," "I want to own my own business," or "I just want to make a good living—maybe six figures one day—and retire nicely." Those goals are fine. But when I ask them what their agenda has to do with God's agenda, I get blank stares.

Why do we act as if God's agenda is hidden or hard to find?

Why does our inability to identify God's will say more about us than it says about God?

We talk about finding God's will, but it's not really lost. God is doing something on earth, and He has very clearly told us about it in Scripture. Our understanding of our ambition has to begin with what God sees as our ambition. If your life isn't part of God's grander purpose, it's a purposeless life, a wasted life, even if you accomplish some really good goals with it.

Identify God's Gifts in You

After Paul recognized the purpose of God, as spelled out in Scripture, he developed an ability to be led by the Spirit of God and learned from the Holy Spirit his specific role in the mission of God. We're designed to proclaim God's glory with our lives and to tell others about it through our witness.

How do you figure out what your specific role is in God's mission? Practice the spiritual gifts you believe you have. Be involved in discipling relationships. One of the best ways to figure out your spiritual gifts is by asking other believers to identify any evidence of them in you. Go on mission trips. They provide a crash course in discovering your gifts. Finally, whatever you're good at, do it well to the glory of God and do it somewhere strategic for the mission of God.

> **What gifts has God given you? What are you passionate about? How could you use this combination of gifts and passion to tell others about Jesus?**

> **What are your hobbies or extracurricular activities? How might you leverage these to share the good news?**

Whatever gifts you have, interpret them in light of the bigger picture of God's purposes stated in His Word: to take the gospel to the ends of the earth.

PRAYER AND REFLECTION

Everyone is called to share the gospel. We owe God our hearts and our obedience. Spend time confessing your love for Him, your thankfulness for His work in your life, and your desire to live on mission with Him. .

ENGAGE WITH YOUR COMMUNITY

The purpose of this section is to help you process key ideas from this week's study with other members of your group. Take some time to thoughtfully consider the following questions. Then record your responses. Reach out to one or two members of your group and discuss your answers together.

This week we're thinking about the role all Christians play in the mission of God. In the first personal study, we saw that God's purpose in the world is to make Himself known and our role in God's purpose is to use our gifts to make Him known. However, to make God known, we must be able to share the way He can be known. We must increase our ability to communicate the gospel message.

To share the gospel, you have to know the gospel. If you had two minutes to share the gospel with someone, what would you say? Record your ideas.

Now that you've written a gospel presentation, find someone to share it with. Record the name of the person with whom you will share.

WHO'S YOUR ONE?

Even though most Christians claim that sharing their faith is important, many more never share their faith with another person. Whether it's because they're afraid or don't know how, many people become uncomfortable when the conversation shifts to matters of faith. Even though worship numbers increasing, baptisms are decreasing.[1] Something needs to change.

Intentional evangelism has always been a defining characteristic of Christian mission, And rightly so, because evangelism is the primary tool by which we fulfill the Great Commission. But as the study showed, we've failed to make evangelism a priority.

> **What role does evangelism play in your faith? What about in the faith of other Christians you know?**

Many Christians feel uncomfortable with the idea of evangelism. Maybe this is because many churches seem to lack a clear evangelism strategy. In the church where I grew up, Wednesday-afternoon soul-winning was a new believer's first act of sanctification! I'm not kidding. I got saved on a Friday and went on my first soul-winning visit the next Wednesday. For various reasons, most churches have discontinued that practice. But what has replaced it? Door-to-door evangelism was the way I learned to share the gospel. Are ordinary Christians equipped to share the gospel? Do they believe it's their responsibility? Are they actually doing it?

> **On the previous page you were asked to record a brief gospel presentation and share it with someone. How did that go? What did you learn?**

> **If you ignored that activity, why did you?**

Our focus on evangelism often seems to have been supplanted or at least downplayed by other good missional initiatives. For instance, church planting is a good practice and should enhance our evangelistic efforts. But what kind of churches are we planting? Are we sending out church planters who know how to set up events that attract bored Christians from other churches, or are we sending out church planters who are committed to discipling and training people to share the gospel?

Why should other good but secondary pursuits never replace the primary calling of evangelism in our lives?

Here are some actions we can take to keep our main focus on evangelism.

Pray for Spiritual Awakening Leading to Action

Historically, revivals haven't begun when lost people were saved but when the church was "reconverted" to the gospel, which then led to massive evangelism. Revival intensifies the normal operations of the Holy Spirit. Until the Spirit comes, all else is futile.

When was the most recent time you prayed for revival? Why should we regularly ask God to work in noticeable ways?

Celebrate the Right Goals

What we celebrate communicates what we value. More than any attendance number, we should want people to know the Lord. Our celebration should match the celebration in heaven:

> *There will be more joy in heaven over one sinner who repents than over ninety-nine righteous people who don't need repentance.*
> **LUKE 15:7**

What good but not ultimate goals do we celebrate instead of repentant sinners' salvation?

Do Whatever It Takes to Reach the Lost

The factors that cause the church to grow don't change in any age: belief in the gospel, commitment to the authority of Scripture, commitment to prayer, and commitment to evangelism. Our ministry should match that of Jesus:

> *The Son of Man has come to seek and to save the lost.*
> **LUKE 19:10**

What was the focus of Jesus' ministry? How closely does your focus match His?

Identify Your One

One year at the Summit Church we asked each member of our congregation to identify one person to pray for and seek to bring to Christ over the year. The phrase we kept repeating was "Who's your one?" It's not an elaborate or complicated plan but a simple idea that led to our most evangelistically fruitful year to date. Because of this intentional effort, we baptized seven hundred people that year. What an incredible joy it was when people said, "Pastor, this is my one!" or when they stood together in the baptistery!

Who's your one? Who are you intentionally praying for? Take a moment to consider who this could be and record their name.

When will you contact this person? What steps could you take to intentionally seek to share the gospel with them?

PRAYER AND REFLECTION

Close your study today by praying for your one. Ask God to graciously and radically deliver them from their sin and bring them into His kingdom.

---

1. Lisa Cannon Green, Worship Attendance Rises, Baptisms Decline in SBC, *Facts & Trends*, June 1, 2018, https://factsandtrends.net/2018/06/01/worship-attendance-rises-baptisms-decline-in-sbc/.

ENGAGE WITH THE WORLD

The purpose of this section is to help you process key ideas from this week's study and think differently about the way you engage with the world. Take some time to thoughtfully consider the following questions. Then record your responses.

Maybe you've already identified your one. But what if there was another "one" living next door or right down the street? What if there was another "one" in the desk next to you at school? To engage with the world, you might just need to look down the street. Maybe God has placed people around you so that He could use you tell them about His grace.

Who are your neighbors? What do you know about them? What would be a good next step to getting to know them?

If you've never met your neighbors, when will you introduce yourself? When could you hang out with them or invite them to do something with your family?

How can you get to know your neighbors without treating them like a project?

What, if any, hesitancies do you have about seeking to know the people around you for the sake of the gospel? Release those hesitancies to God in prayer.

What would it take for your family to commit to having at least one unbeliever in your house each month?

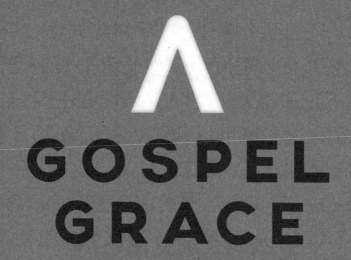

GOSPEL
GRACE

START

Welcome to group session 5 of Gospel Above All.

What were the most challenging and helpful things you learned in last week's study? Why?

What do you think Christians are known for today? Explain.

Hostility toward Christianity is growing in our culture, but this is no time to despair. The early church didn't grow exponentially because the government was behind them but because they trusted the Spirit and boldly proclaimed the gospel. They took the commands Jesus gave them—to love their neighbors and take the gospel to all people (Matt. 22:39; 28:19-20)—and turned the world upside down. We must strive to demonstrate the same attributes Jesus embodied in His ministry: being "full of grace and truth" (John 1:14).

Last week we talked about the need to share the gospel with our friends and neighbors. This week we'll look at the type of people we should be as we seek to share.

WATCH

Refer to this viewer guide as you watch video session 5.

Truth without grace is _____fundamentalism_____. Grace without truth is just _____sentamentality_____.

Your neighbors don't think they need _____saving_____ from their sin. They think they need _____saving_____ from you.

Your _____words_____ can never be stronger than your _____relationships_____.

In Christ you have God's _____kind_____ company that _____redeems_____ not only your soul but also gives you a meaning and a purpose and a grace within that trial.

The first thing lost people think about us is _____condemnation_____, not _____compassion_____.

When you ask _____Jesus_____ to enter a conversation with an unbeliever at the table, it's not to _____stop_____ the conversation. It's to _____enrich_____ it.

Take Notes:

The art of neighboring

DISCUSS

Use the following questions to discuss the video teaching.

Read John 1:14.

*The Word became flesh and dwelt among us. We observed his glory,
the glory as the one and only Son from the Father, full of grace and truth.*

JOHN 1:14

**Jesus had a ministry filled with both grace and truth. Where in
Scripture do we see both at work? What happens when these
attributes are out of balance in our ministries?**

Truth without grace is fundamentalism. Grace without truth is sentimentality.
Fundamentalism refers to elevating minor points of doctrine to ultimate
status. We fall into sentimentality when we let how we feel dictate what
we believe. Jesus possessed grace and truth in equal measure. He was so
concerned with our souls that He left the comforts of heaven to come and give
both grace and truth to a broken and hurting world.

**Read John 4:1-26. How do you see Jesus express grace and truth
in His interaction with the woman at the well? What can we learn
from the way He treated her?**

In this account we see grace and truth in balance. Jesus approached this
woman, entered a conversation with her, asked her for a favor, and spoke
to her heart. At the same time, He didn't hesitate to speak the truth. He
confronted her when necessary, but this confrontation came within a context
that let her know He cared. Our interactions with nonbelievers need to reflect
the balance of grace and truth Jesus expressed.

In a world that's increasingly hostile to the gospel, grace needs to precede
truth in our conversations with people who've rejected Jesus, because our
words will never be stronger than our relationships.

**How does having a personal relationship with someone impact
how they receive what you have to say?**

**How could changing the way you approach lost people open up
gospel opportunities for you?**

A simple change you can make that shows people you care is to be available. Most of us are over-scheduled and tired. Maybe the most obvious and correctable way to be more gracious is simply to make yourself available to people. Because openness is uncommon in our culture, it stands out. Being willing to be present with someone may be all that's needed for a meaningful conversation to occur. As Christians, we need to be known for the same kind of compassion that characterized our Savior.

What are a few ways you can serve in your neighborhood or your larger community?

In the video, Vance Pitman and Rosaria Butterfield described ways they've served their communities. Before people care about what you know, they need to know you care. Acts of service break down boundaries and allow us to enter places we may never have gone before. This enables people to encounter the grace of Christ in the lives of His people.

Share about a time when you helped or served someone. How did that impact your relationship or create opportunities for deeper conversation?

RESPOND

Use these questions to apply today's teaching.

This session's video captured the perspectives of two believers who are showing the love of Christ from two completely different backgrounds. Yet both are committed to embodying the grace and truth of Jesus in order to care for the people around them.

> **The speakers on this session's video shared their experiences forming relationships with people who are far from God. What do you think keeps us from developing relationships this way?**

> **What changes could you make to care for and show love to friends, classmates, or family members who are not Christians?**

PRAYER

Close the session with prayer.

Pray that God will help the members of your group become ministers of Jesus' grace and truth. Ask the Holy Spirit to soften your hearts to the people around you, to give you the supernatural ability to see their needs, and to enable you to love them as He does.

Remind group members to complete these week's personal study.

THE CHURCH IS GOD'S PLAN A

John 17 contains the last recorded prayer Jesus prayed the night before He died. First He prayed for Himself and then for His disciples. Next He did something that may surprise you:

> *I pray not only for these, but also for those who believe in me through their word. May they all be one, as you, Father, are in me and I am in you. May they also be in us, so that the world may believe you sent me. I have given them the glory you have given me, so that they may be one as we are one. I am in them and you are in me, so that they may be made completely one, that the world may know you have sent me and have loved them as you have loved me.*
>
> **JOHN 17:20-23**

Jesus didn't pray for the world but instead for the believers in the world. That may seem selfish. Or maybe it seems as if Jesus doesn't care about the world. But we know Jesus cared so much about the world that He came into the world to save it (John 3:16).

Why did Jesus pray just for the believers and not for the whole world? Because the hope for any community is found in the believers in that community. The church is God's plan A for carrying out God's mission in the world. There is no plan B.

For this reason, believers must be as concerned about our disposition as our position. Truth is important to Christians, and that's a good thing. Earlier in this same prayer Jesus asked that believers would be sanctified in the truth (17:17). But John's Gospel also tells us that Jesus was "full of grace and truth" (1:14). Unfortunately, many Christians are more concerned with truth at the expense of grace.

How do think most teenagers in your community view Christians? Do these opinions have more to do with the beliefs we hold or the manner with which we express them?

How closely does your attitude toward others match Jesus'?

We shouldn't miss the fact that Jesus prayed for us to internalize God's love in His final prayer (17:23). He prayed for us to love Jesus the way God loves Jesus and love other people the way Jesus loves us (vv. 24-25). When we love as Jesus loves, people will know He's real. Particularly in a time of cultural upheaval, the church needs to be known as gracious and loving, because the love of the church makes the love of Christ visible to the community.

The church's love shows itself to unbelievers in two primary ways.

In the Way We Serve Our Community

We are not proclaiming ourselves but Jesus Christ as Lord, and ourselves as your servants for Jesus's sake.
2 CORINTHIANS 4:5

If anyone wants to be first, he must be last and servant of all.
MARK 9:35

How could our willingness to serve our community make someone more willing to hear the message of the gospel? How does our service authenticate Christ's work in our hearts?

What opportunities exist through your church to serve your community? How do you participate in service?

When we love people who can't pay us back, we show that God is at work among us. When we engage in seemingly mundane, ordinary acts of kindness, we show our community that we care. When we care for the vulnerable and the orphan, love prisoners, serve refugees, and befriend political enemies, we make Jesus visible. Service is an identifying mark of a disciple because the work of the servant reflects the will of the Master.

In the Unity That Binds Us Together

*By this everyone will know that you are my
disciples, if you love one another.*

JOHN 13:35

The church should be a place where the love of Christ is always evident.
Love is evident in unity. When we lose our unity in the church, it's because
something has become more important to us than Jesus. We need to be
careful about the way we interact with people, both personally and on social
media. Our tone matters, and we always want to communicate in ways that
show the gospel of grace at work in our lives.

**If the world will know Jesus by the way we love other Christians,
what do we communicate if we're unloving?**

*We're communicating that there isn't any forgiveness or
love in the Gospel*

When we express our perspective, we should do so with a spirit of love, grace,
and unity, declaring that the blessing of knowing Jesus is greater than any
opinions we have about less important matters. In nonessential matters, we
need to extend charity.

If we live in loving unity, as Jesus prayed we would, our evangelism efforts will
become much more effective. We won't have to invite people to come to our
church. They'll beat down the doors to come and see what's going on: "Who's
this powerful superhero who once walked the earth who fills your church with
love and grace and truth?" Then we can tell them about Jesus.

PRAYER AND REFLECTION

Evaluate your social-media communication and your conversations over
the past week. Have you written or said anything that's less than loving
or gracious? What posts do you need to delete? What apologies do you
need to make? Close with a prayer for grace to be effective in your group.

ENGAGE WITH YOUR COMMUNITY

Take some time to thoughtfully consider the following questions. Then reach out to one or two people from your group and discuss your answers together.

At the heart of our desire to be a gracious, loving people is a desire for people to know and believe the gospel. Read what Paul said about the attitude of someone who seeks to share the gospel:

Devote yourselves to prayer; stay alert in it with thanksgiving. At the same time, pray also for us that God may open a door to us for the word, to speak the mystery of Christ, for which I am in chains, so that I may make it known as I should. Act wisely toward outsiders, making the most of the time. Let your speech always be gracious, seasoned with salt, so that you may know how you should answer each person.

COLOSSIANS 4:2-6

According to Paul, how should we prepare for gospel opportunities? List as many commands as you can find.

Devote ourselves to prayer, act wisely, let our speech be gracious

How do our actions and our speech positively or negatively influence our witness?

Where do you think Christians most often fail to communicate truth graciously? What do you personally need to work on to become more gracious?

DO NOT JUDGE

Even though Christians may be as gracious as possible, they'll still be considered judgmental by the nonbelievers around them. "Do not judge" (Matt. 7:1) is one of the most popular Bible verses in our society, especially among non-Christians. It seems to fit in with two of our society's most basic assumptions: that religion is private and that morality is relative. People love "Do not judge" because it's a handy way of saying, "You can't tell me I'm wrong." Begin to make a public assessment of almost any moral issue, and this verse will swiftly be pulled out as a deflective weapon.

In what context have you heard someone say, "Do not judge"?

Does this verse mean we should never offer an opinion? Explain.

The problem is, Jesus—the One who spoke these words—didn't share our society's assumptions about private religion and relative morality. He constantly made public judgments, many of them rather striking. In John 7:7 He told His disciples that the world hated Him "because I testify about it— that its works are evil." So what did Jesus mean, and how should we take it to heart?

The type of judging Jesus warns against occurs not when you assess their position but when you dismiss them as a person. There's a difference between speaking a hard truth and condemning a person. Condemning goes beyond saying, "This position is wrong" to saying, "I don't want you around anymore." The antidote to judging is to remember the gospel. Here are some signs that you've forgotten the gospel and have started judging other people.

You're more enraged by someone else's sin than you're embarrassed by your own. After Jesus told us not to judge, He added helpful context, saying we would be hypocrites to point out the splinter in someone else's eye without removing the log in our own (Matt. 7:3-5).To confront others in their sin, we need to be painfully aware of our own.

Why should our sin be more obvious to us than others' sins?

If it isn't, we start to think too highly of ourselves

You refuse to forgive. To refuse to forgive someone is to be almost entirely ignorant of the enormity of what God has forgiven you of. It's just another way of saying, "I'm constantly going to remind you of this offense and use it as an excuse for treating you with contempt." In contrast, forgiveness means absorbing the debt and offering love and goodness in return.

Do you need to forgive or receive forgiveness from anyone?

You cut off relationships with people who disagree with you. As a Christian, you have to love another person more than you love your position on a particular issue. That doesn't mean you ever compromise your position or fail to state it. But it means you remain committed to loving the people who passionately disagree with you.

We need to listen to people to make sure we understand their positions. Why would this be an important step in being gracious to one another?

You gossip. What makes gossip so dangerous is that you judge someone without giving them a chance to change. At least if you judged someone to their face, they could do something about it. And don't mask gossip with a "prayer request" or a phrase like "I am not trying to throw shade but . . . ."

Why do we treat gossip as a respectable or excusable sin? Why does gossiping or listening to gossip show a lack of God's grace in our lives?

You refuse to receive criticism. Why do you hate criticism? Isn't it because you hate to admit that you have faults? But if you understand the gospel, that idea shouldn't surprise you. So when others point out your sin you should be able to say, "Well, of course. In fact, I could tell you some other shortcomings you didn't notice."

When was the most recent time you received criticism? How did you respond?

You refuse to correct someone's position. Irony alert! As a Christian, when you refuse to correct someone, it's for one of two reasons: you don't believe the Bible is true or you don't think the other person can actually change. But by assuming the other person won't change and won't listen, you're judging and condemning them from the start. You're consigning them to their sin without ever giving them a chance to receive grace.

You write someone off as hopeless. We serve a Savior who raises the dead. If we keep our mouths shut because we think someone is beyond hope—or worse, if we're just afraid of an awkward interaction—we're saying we would rather our friends suffer the full consequences of their sins than speak a word of warning and correction.

Why is telling someone about Jesus the most gracious thing we can do for them?

Notice the balance between grace and truth. Don't judge others by withholding the truth, but don't judge them by speaking the truth without grace. Truth without grace is judgmental fundamentalism. Grace without truth is liberal sentimentality. People need both the grace and the truth of the gospel.

Review the signs of a judgmental spirit. How do you need to grow in gospel grace and truth? Why?

PRAYER AND REFLECTION

Read 1 Corinthians 13. As you read, ask God to mold your love into the character of love described in His Word.

ENGAGE WITH THE WORLD

The purpose of this section is to help you process key ideas from this week's study and think differently about the way you engage with the world. Take some time to thoughtfully consider the following questions. Then record your responses.

Spend some concentrated time with someone who isn't yet a follower of Jesus and ask him or her these questions. Try to listen closely to the responses without giving much feedback. Record the person's responses and your thoughts.

Ask someone who isn't a believer how they think of Christians.

Ask what ideas inform their perception and opinion of Christians.

What elements of their critique do you need to take to heart or follow up on?

GOSPEL
COMMUNITY

START

Welcome to group session 6 of Gospel Above All.

This week we'll explore what kind of community the gospel creates—one where all kinds of people are welcome.

Have you ever spent significant time in a culture different from your own? What did you learn from that experience?

Our mission isn't to reach only one kind of person but all kinds of people. Therefore, Christian community needs to find its unity not in cultural conformity but in the gospel, which supersedes all cultures. One indication that God is at work in a group is the diversity of background, age, ethnicity, socioeconomic status, and other cultural characteristics. A gospel community is willing to be uncomfortable and set aside preferences to win souls.

WATCH

Refer to this viewer guide as you watch video session 6.

Stages in Multicultural Growth

1. _____Ignorance_____

2. _____Awareness_____

3. _____Intentionality_____

4. _____Gospel_____ _____Community_____

If we look at a multicultural people of God, we're looking at a group of people who have had to put someone ___before___ themselves, be humble to hear someone's experience, and to ___act___ on it.

We have to exhibit the ___characteristics___ of Christ in ways we haven't had to before, in ___circumstances___ we haven't had to apply them to.

___Proximity___ breeds ___empathy___.

There's a fabric of the image of God woven into every ___culture___, and it's only when you see all of those cultures together in the ultimate kingdom around the throne of Jesus that you see the ___full___ ___expression___ of the image of God in the body of Christ.

Take Notes:

DISCUSS

Use the following content to discuss the video teaching.

The gospel creates a multicultural community, which is different from a multicolored community. Clearly, having people of different ethnicities in our churches is a blessing, but the gospel goes beyond this level of diversity. Being multicultural is a much broader concept, meaning multiple cultures are expressed and represented in our churches.

> **What expressions of worship or church order have you assumed to be the right way but are actually just cultural preferences?**

God is equally honored through different preferences in church practice. We must be careful not to assume that the way we worship is inherently more biblical than the way another culture worships. Differences in music, prayer, preaching style, and the order of services come more from our preferences than from what the Bible prescribes. Being willing to forsake some of our preferences in church practice allows us to reach beyond our primary culture.

> **What happens when we take our preferences and elevate them to the level of nonnegotiable truths?**

> **The speakers in this video session pointed out that our experience determines our preferences and the way we approach a Bible text. How could becoming more multicultural help us appreciate the Bible more?**

All of the New Testament letters deal with issues that stem from cultural preferences. Our cultural identity shapes how we live in dozens of ways. This fact extends to life in the body of Christ. God loves people from every culture, and there are aspects of every culture that glorify God. When we expand our community, we have the privilege of learning more about the God we serve, the people who bear His image, and the Word that communicates His heart.

> **How diverse is your network of relationships? What keeps us from living multicultural lives?**

> **Read 2 Corinthians 5:16. How does our identity in Christ reshape the way we see other people?**

Christ's mission can't be completed unless we're willing to cross cultural boundaries. Doing so requires intentional action and growth on the part of all Christians. The reason we don't have multicultural churches is that we don't lead multicultural lives. When we find our identity in Christ, that should lead us to expand our communities rather than restrict them. Because the gospel is for every culture, we must befriend and love people from every culture.

Read 1 Corinthians 9:19-23. What kind of effort will be required to expand the diversity our communities?

If we want to live multicultural lives we must forgo preferences in nonessential matters, such as the order of worship or the style of music or preaching, for the sake of others. We must allow others to teach us their perspectives on what it means to follow Jesus. This process doesn't happen by accident; we have to humble ourselves and work at it.

Of the suggestions given on the video for developing multicultural lives, which ones could you put into practice in your church and in your life?

God's coming kingdom will be a people of all ethnicities and cultures united around God's throne in worship (Rev. 7:9-10). Although our churches can't match the diversity of heaven, we should strive to reflect, at a minimum, the diversity of our community around our churches. Our willingness to come together across differences and celebrate the one Savior of all shows that we've placed the gospel above all.

RESPOND

Use these questions to apply today's teaching.

> *I will bring them to my holy mountain*
> *and let them rejoice in my house of prayer.*
> *Their burnt offerings and sacrifices*
> *will be acceptable on my altar,*
> *for my house will be called a house of prayer*
> *for all nations.*
>
> **ISAIAH 56:7**

Jesus quoted this verse, saying His house would be "a house of prayer for all nations" (Mark 11:17). In the video, Walter Strickland suggested we pray for cultures and ethnicities that aren't our own. Vance Pitman said prayer transcends cultures. If we find that our culture is lacking in diversity or if we are rigidly unwilling to learn from other cultures, it's time to pray.

> **What are some ways you can pray for your own culture and others with whom you come into contact?**
>
> **What's one way you'd like to grow in your understanding of others? Pray about these matters.**

PRAYER

Close the session with prayer.

Father God, thank You for calling people from every nation to know You, worship You, and serve You. We ask that You'll help us consider ways we can begin to develop multicultural lives. We know this change might make us uncomfortable and may require us to alter our preferences, but we know the glory of Your name is worth the sacrifice. Amen.

Remind group members to complete this week's personal study.

MULTICULTURAL MORE THAN MULTICOLORED

Describe your experience in church. Have you typically gone to a church with people who look like you? If so, why?

Most churches say they want to be diverse, but it wasn't until recently that I began to see the difference between two types of diversity: multicolored and multicultural. Many churches have people of different ethnicities, but because the church culture is still predominantly white, everyone sings traditional white-people music and sits silently during the sermon. In many contexts, having a multicolored congregation is a step that should be celebrated. Having church members from different ethnic backgrounds is miles ahead of a church that has no ethnic diversity at all, but this multicolored diversity is only skin deep.

However, in a multicultural church diversity is celebrated. A variety of groups influence worship, so more "Amens!" might be heard during the sermon than white people are accustomed to. Changes like this may be uncomfortable for a lot of members, but that discomfort is actually a sign that the church is multicultural. A multicultural church causes people to feel a little uncomfortable because it incorporates practices outside the predominant culture. If you're always comfortable at your church, that comfort is probably a sign that your church reflects only your culture.

What would you say your preferences are for a church service? Which of those are based merely on personal preferences?

Why should you be willing to forgo preferences in worship and church practice to cultivate broader diversity in your congregation?

Because God is involved in culture, every culture has something to celebrate. A multicolored church looks like a salad; different elements exist in close proximity, but each piece is still distinct in color and never takes on the characteristics of the others. But a multicultural church is more like beef stew; multiple ingredients come together, sharing what makes them unique and bringing out one another's distinct flavors. The result is more than the mere sum of its parts.

For many churches, the biggest hurdle to becoming multicultural isn't theological but preferential. If we change our style to make our church more accessible to nonwhites, as I believe we should, a lot of white people will simply dislike it. Sadly, that means we'll reach a lot fewer of them. Ultimately, we'd love for people to overcome their personal preferences. But we can't always expect people to be mature before we reach them, so change has to be gradual in most instances. The goal is to reach the point where people are comfortable being uncomfortable.

How do we grow in our ability to distinguish a gospel distinctive from a cultural distinctive?

Why do we have a tendency to confuse the two? How have you noticed this tendency in your life?

Read 1 Corinthians 9:19-23.

Although I am free from all and not anyone's slave, I have made myself a slave to everyone, in order to win more people. To the Jews I became like a Jew, to win Jews; to those under the law, like one under the law—though I myself am not under the law—to win those under the law. To those who are without the law, like one without the law—though I am not without God's law but under the law of Christ—to win those without the law. To the weak I became weak, in order to win the weak. I have become all things to all people, so that I may by every possible means save some. Now I do all this because of the gospel, so that I may share in the blessings.

1 CORINTHIANS 9:19-23

How did Paul value his heritage as a Jew? What made Paul willing to lay aside that heritage?

How does the gospel allow us both to celebrate our own culture and appreciate other cultures?

Paul was a Jew by birth. He never lost his cultural heritage, but he was willing to lay aside some of it to pursue gospel growth among the Gentiles.

I will never lose my ethnic background as a white country boy any more than my African-American neighbor will lose his. But our Christian identity must be weightier to us than our ethnic identity or preferences. Uniting on that basis allows us to appreciate our ethnic diversity instead of fearing it. Our purpose in being a multicultural congregation isn't to create one culture-free race and label it Christian but to retain and celebrate our heritage while recognizing that our identity in Christ outweighs it. Ethnicity is and should be important to us, but it must never be as weighty as our identity in Christ.

How do we reach the point at which the gospel determines our preferences?

The redemption Jesus purchased for us wasn't merely individual salvation; it was also interpersonal, intercultural, interracial salvation. When the world sees God bringing together what sin has driven apart, they'll cry out with amazement, "Surely God is among you!"

PRAYER AND REFLECTION

Evaluate your preferences. Which should you be willing to forgo for the sake of greater gospel-focused diversity? Ask God to give you a desire to see His body grow across traditional ethnic dividing lines.

ENGAGE WITH YOUR COMMUNITY

The purpose of this section is to help you process key ideas from this week's study with other members of your group. Take some time to thoughtfully consider the following questions. Then record your responses. Reach out to one or two members of your group and discuss your answers together.

Are your friendships filled with people who look like you? If so, why?

If not, what have you learned from diverse cultural expression? How have those experiences challenged you?

Would you describe your church at multicolored, multicultured, or neither? Why? How could you help move your church toward broader diversity?

AWARENESS ISN'T ENOUGH

In the first personal study we examined the idea of identity. What are some ways you would identify yourself?

How does the gospel change or reshape every part of that identity?

The church I pastor seeks to be a church that reflects the diversity of its community and declares the diversity of the kingdom. As we've made strides in becoming multicultural, one of the biggest lessons we've learned is that an awareness of a society composed of different ethnicities, while absolutely vital, isn't enough to make diversity a reality. One of our African-American pastors, Chris Green, uses the following spectrum to summarize the process by which a church becomes racially diverse.

Before we evaluate these stages, mark your church's position on the spectrum.

Ignorance	Awareness	Interaction	Gospel community

Ignorance. We all start here. Most of us grow up around people like us, work with people like us, and socialize with people like us. We aren't willfully hateful, but we simply don't know much about people from different backgrounds. So we—especially those of us in the majority culture—fill in the gaps with assumptions and stereotypes. We assume black people or Hispanic people all think, act, or feel a certain way.

Awareness. Admitting our ignorance of other cultures leads us to the next step on the spectrum: awareness. Perhaps we watch a news story on TV, make a new friend, or have a personal experience that forces us to recognize cultural differences. Awareness is unsettling because it challenges a lot of what we assumed was simply normal.

Why is admitting our ignorance so difficult for us? Why is it necessary if we seek to grow?

Interaction. Once we reach awareness, we often declare success. Acknowledging other cultures isn't enough. The jump from awareness to interaction really begins to change the game. Only when we develop personal relationships with people from other ethnicities and backgrounds, seek to understand them, grow to respect them, and learn from them can we move closer to true community.

Gospel community. Reaching this stage requires dedicated intentionality: to have people from diverse backgrounds in our lives, to ask questions and listen, to humble ourselves and ask for forgiveness. But it's worth it—for Jesus' sake, for His church's sake, and for our own sake. Cultivating gospel community isn't something we do merely as an act of grace for others. We need it for our own souls as well.

To have interaction, we must be around people who are different from us. When were you most recently around people who are different from you?

If your circles of friendship lack diversity, what could you do to meet or get to know people outside your immediate culture?

Interpersonal connection is more important than finding a worship style that people of all different backgrounds and cultures will all like. (Good luck with that.) God didn't call us to put on a multicultural display on the weekend but to live out a multicultural wonder throughout the week. As believers united in Christ, we aren't pursuing sameness but a covenant community of oneness.

The power to pursue this kind of unity is found only in the gospel. As Christians, we can offer something our society can only dream of. Our society wants us to be aware, but it can't offer a way for us to love one another like family. However, we in the church know we're a family—black, white, Latino, Asian, Arab, and every other ethnic group that God has lovingly created. Only the gospel can create and unite this family. As the old saying goes, the ground is level at the foot of the cross.

The gospel doesn't drive a wedge between different cultures; it celebrates them. The gospel is the only reality that creates a new race that's neither black nor white, neither Asian nor Arab, but a new race designated Christian (Eph 2:11-22). Unity among diversity thrives in the church of Jesus Christ:

> *There is no Jew or Greek, slave or free, male and*
> *female; since you are all one in Christ Jesus.*
> **GALATIANS 3:28**

This kind of unity turned heads when Christianity first burst onto the scene in the first century. And if we pursue multicultural lives, it will turn heads again.

No matter how different you may be from other brothers and sisters in Christ, what will you and other believers always have in common in Christ?

Look back at the spectrum on page 88. What's one step you can take to move to the next stage on the spectrum?

PRAYER AND REFLECTION

Ask God to show you how you can move beyond awareness to a true community with people of different backgrounds, ethnicities, and socioeconomic levels. Pray for the grace and patience required for this change to occur.

ENGAGE WITH THE WORLD

The purpose of this section is to help you process key ideas from this week's study and think differently about the way you engage with the world. Take some time to thoughtfully consider the following questions. Then record your responses.

Sometimes we need to step outside our comfort zone.
What cultures are represented in your community?

How could you immerse yourself in a different culture
for even a couple of hours? This culture might
be racial, socioeconomic, or religious.

Record what you learned from associating
with another culture. What preferences did
you find that are different from yours?

GOSPEL
UNITY

START

Welcome to group session 7 of Gospel Above All.

In light of last week's study of gospel community, have you identified any preferences you need to reconsider for the sake of others?

You've probably heard it said that we shouldn't talk about religion and politics in polite conversation. Why do you think we're told these conversations should be off-limits?

Today's cultural and political landscape changes at a breakneck pace. While Jesus was on earth, He was careful not to become involved in matters that didn't directly pertain to His work and ministry. Getting involved in every political concern keeps us from giving our primary focus to the work of the gospel. There's room in the church for people with different political beliefs, but to keep the gospel above all, we need to filter everything we do through the Great Commission.

WATCH

Refer to this viewer guide as you watch video session 7.

I don't want to engage in _____ in any kind of way that would cause me to be weaker as a minister of the _____ of Jesus Christ.

We're talking about the saving message of salvation that comes through the substitutionary atonement of Jesus Christ and makes it possible for _____ to be saved and given the gift of _____ _____.

Christians are coming into the body of Christ from _____ places.

The Scripture will not _____ a candidate. The Scripture will show where there are common principles, but it will also show where the kingdom of God is _____ and _____.

When politics deals with allegiance and loyalty, there is nothing more _____ about allegiance and loyalty than the claim that Jesus Christ is _____.

If politics is _____ to you, then Jesus Christ isn't Lord to you. If politics is _____ to you, you're not obeying Christ when He says, "Love God and love your neighbor as yourself."

To be a follower of Jesus, I enter this conversation with _____ and _____.

The thing that has hurt Bible-believing Christianity the most regarding our unity has been a lack of _____, and _____ to the pain of others.

We can't expect to have a _____ political discussion without having _____ people.

ANSWERS: politics, gospel / sinners, eternal life /different / endorse, different, unique / fundamental, Lord / ultimate, unimportant / empathy, charity / sensitivity, indifference / Christian, Christlike

DISCUSS

Use the following questions to discuss the video teaching.

Being a gospel witness is more important than any political stand we take. When we enter political discussions, our primary concern should be to refrain from anything harmful to our witness for the gospel. Should we take an unpopular stand on moral issues? Absolutely, but our discourse and actions must be covered in grace.

> **What does it look like to disagree gracefully? Whom do you know who has modeled this skill? What opportunities do Christians have in our culture of perpetual outrage?**
>
> **Read Romans 12:18. How can we maintain a disposition of grace and humility when our stand on issues causes people to assume we're hateful or intolerant?**

As Kevin Smith said on the video, we want to share the gospel with sinners, so we don't want to alienate them through our political engagement when possible. When the gospel is a priority in our decision making, it drives the way we vote and advocate.

Although Scripture doesn't explicitly address many issues we face when engaging with our culture, it provides principles that can help equip us to make God-honoring decisions and respond lovingly to moral issues. No matter how we're perceived or received, we can respond with grace, whether the issue is incredibly clear morally or one about which Christians of good conscience disagree.

> **How do biblical principles help shape our positions on issues that Scripture doesn't clearly address? What are some examples of these principles?**

The Bible speaks on many issues very clearly. We should care for the poor, advocate for the vulnerable, uphold the institution of marriage, protect children, and value the dignity of work, among other stances. Even if we passionately care about an issue, the way our passion translates into policy is often less clear. We get ourselves in trouble when we assume our position on an issue is God's position on the same issue.

What did Albert Mohler mean on the video when he said we should be careful about using the word Christian as a modifier?

Why is it so easy for us to replace our identity as followers of Jesus Christ with a political affiliation or position? How do we actively resist this temptation?

There's no single Christian policy for taxes, the economy, or foreign policy. Therefore, the word *Christian* can't adequately describe a policy; it describes who we are as the redeemed people of God. The gospel provides us with our ultimate identity. All other identities and loyalties are subservient to that. We don't have to look to any issue to provide us with identity or purpose. We find those in our designation as sons and daughters of God. Although we're free to engage with a variety of moral and social issues, they'll never become the ultimate identifiers of who we are as followers of Christ.

Read Jude 3; Philippians 3:14; Ephesians 4:3. How do these passages shape the way we relate to and consider one another, particularly in our politics?

How can we focus our energy on unity in Christ despite political differences?

RESPOND

Use these questions to apply today's teaching.

The gospel guides our political engagement, and gospel-minded Christians can disagree on a variety of issues without compromising the gospel. Our witness to the gospel must come before every other priority.

> **How can we be sure we value the gospel above all else, including political and social issues?**

> **Do you need to reconsider the way you've approached politics? How will you approach politics differently in the future?**

PRAYER

Close the session with prayer.

Scripture calls us to pray for our government leaders, specifically so that we can have an environment in which the gospel can flourish. Close your time together by praying these verses:

> *First of all, then, I urge that petitions, prayers, intercessions, and thanksgivings be made for everyone, for kings and all those who are in authority, so that we may lead a tranquil and quiet life in all godliness and dignity. This is good, and it pleases God our Savior, who wants everyone to be saved and to come to the knowledge of the truth.*
> **1 TIMOTHY 2:1-4**

Remind group members to complete this week's personal study.

FOUR MYTHS ABOUT CHRISTIAN POLITICAL ENGAGEMENT, PART 1

Political engagement has always been a tough subject for me. I often feel guilty for not doing more. Doesn't obedience require standing up for truth and justice? But, as a Christian leader, I also often feel guilty for having said too much. Am I putting unnecessary obstacles in the way of the gospel?

If you don't struggle with that tension, you've probably fallen into a ditch on one of two sides, either investing politics with too much weight or not enough.

Which side of the ditch do you most often fall in? Investing too much or too little in politics or social issues? Explain.

It's easy for Christians to look at politics and want to walk away altogether. It's much harder—and much more necessary—to engage in politics as one way of influencing our society. The question is: How do we engage in politics without compromising the gospel? Or conversely how do we engage in politics and social issues in a way that prizes the gospel above all else? To answer these two questions, let's examine four myths about political engagement Christians must reject.

Myth 1: Secondary Political Ideals Are Matters of First Importance

There are two reasons politics has to be secondary for believers.

1. We might be wrong about some political issues. It would be a tragedy to let an error on a secondary issue obscure our testimony about the gospel. I may be wrong about my economic views, but I know I'm not wrong about the gospel. I don't want my opinion on the former to prevent people from hearing the latter.

2. Even if we're right about an issue, politics simply doesn't matter as much as the gospel. Naturally, there are causes we should advocate

for. However, what matters above all else is that we're known as gospel people.

List three political issues about which Christians might disagree in good conscience.

1.

2.

3.

Read Matthew 10:2-4. How are Matthew and Simon described?

Matthew the _____

Simon the _____

Learn a lesson from Jesus' disciples. In the same group were Matthew the tax collector (part of the current political establishment) and Simon the Zealot (someone radically opposed to the current establishment). The Gospels never indicate that they abandoned their political views. They found unity in Christ that superseded their differences.

What can we learn from Jesus' willingness to include people from two radically different viewpoints in His inner circle?

Jesus willingly sought out people of opposing viewpoints. Is this true of you? Why or why not?

Read Daniel 1:8-21. How did Daniel put his faithfulness to God before political matters? What can you learn from his example?

Myth 2: Christian Truth Doesn't Apply to Politics

The freedoms we enjoy as a nation don't stand as isolated ideals. They all sprang from the work of generations of Christians who were engaged in the political process.

What are some political positions you hold that are rooted in your faith as a follower of Jesus?

Think about Christians who feel different from you about certain issues. How could their convictions be rooted in their faith?

Even our Constitution grounds the rights and freedoms of individuals not in the will of people but in the will of the Creator. As I've heard it said, "Democracy is two wolves and a lamb voting on what to have for lunch. Liberty is the lamb having grounds, before God, on which to contest the vote." There must be something more than the voice of the majority, and that something is the voice of God.

That's why Martin Luther King Jr. had the authority to say the American majority was wrong in the way it treated black men and women. Racism was written into the law of the land, but King said it violated a higher law—the law of the Creator.

We must never give up that conviction. Even when our society encourages us to leave our Christian convictions at the door, we must politely and firmly resist. The Christian worldview has implications for all of life, so we've got to apply it to all of life.

PRAYER AND REFLECTION

Pray about the deep divisions in our culture on political issues. Ask the Holy Spirit to give the church the supernatural ability to be a balm that brings healing in our current atmosphere of conflict.

ENGAGE WITH YOUR COMMUNITY

The purpose of this section is to help you process key ideas from this week's study with other members of your group. Take some time to thoughtfully consider the following questions. Then record your responses. Reach out to one or two members of your group and discuss your answers together.

In politics it's easy to demonize people we don't understand. Twenty-four-hour-a-day cable news and social media have created an echo chamber that exposes us only to our own viewpoint, creating the illusion that our views seem more prevalent than they actually are. To disagree with someone in a Christlike way, we need to understand their position and be able to describe what they believe in a way that would be recognizable to them. To develop this ability, we need to speak to people who are different from us.

Who's a brother or sister in Christ with a
different political viewpoint from you?

Have a conversation with that person, learn how they have
come to their position, and record what you learned.

How do your different viewpoints lead you both to serve Christ?

FOUR MYTHS ABOUT CHRISTIAN POLITICAL ENGAGEMENT, PART 2

In the previous personal study, we examined the first two of four myths about Christian political engagement. In this study, we'll consider the other two myths.

> **What did you find most helpful or most challenging in the previous personal study?**

Myth 3: There's Never a Time to Take a Controversial Political Stand

Many Christian leaders hesitate to be vocal about political issues because they don't want to become "those people." You know the ones. You've already blocked their posts on social media because everything they say is political … and outraged. But a time comes when we must speak. As Dietrich Bonhoeffer learned in the 1930s and '40s, there's a marked difference between saying, "Discrimination is wrong" and saying, "We must oppose the Nazi Party."

Think about John the Baptist. He publicly criticized Herod's sexual ethics and lost his head for it. I can imagine the bloggers of his day whispering to one another, "If he had just stuck with love and grace, he'd still be alive." But what was Jesus' assessment of John? The greatest prophet ever (Luke 7:28). We must speak uncomfortable, unpopular truths, even if it means following the path of John the Baptist.

> **What's an example of a controversial stand worth taking? Why should we take these stands despite the cost?**

> **How can we discern when to speak up and when not to?**

Thinking about your own political engagement, should you speak up more or less? Why?

We also need to remember not every controversial political stance rises to the same level of importance. We must develop the discernment to decide when we don't need to take a stand. Jesus' ministry provides an example.

Read Luke 12:13-21. What was the man asking Jesus to do? How did Jesus respond? Why did Jesus respond this way?

What did Jesus mean when He said His kingdom was "not of this world" (John 18:36)?

When people asked Jesus a specific social-justice question, He refused to judge: "Who appointed me a judge or arbitrator over you?" (Luke 12:14). It's not because He didn't care about justice or wouldn't have been able to offer wise counsel. Rather, Jesus rules over a kingdom that's not of this world. Although many of His followers expected Him to be a political leader, He rejected that label. He avoided giving an opinion in this particular case, instead preaching a sermon on greed, the source of the conflict (vv. 15-21). We're limited in our perspective, and that reality leads to the final myth.

Myth 4: We See Every Issue Clearly

Have you ever changed your mind on a political issue? If so, why?

Faithful Christians can be wrong. As sinful people, we should expect to be wrong. It is embarrassing to read about American pastors in the past who claimed a "Scriptural" basis for African slavery. But these grave mistakes shouldn't surprise us. Each one of us is more deeply shaped by our culture than we'll ever know.

However, the glaring errors of our spiritual ancestors shouldn't lead us to arrogance. I often hear remarks like "Can you believe how backward they were?" The implication is "Thank God we're so sophisticated and have it figured out." Yes, our ancestors were wrong on many points. They had blind spots. But so do we. The proper attitude to take isn't one of pride but one of profound humility. We don't see every issue clearly.

Read Matthew 5:13-16. Even though we don't see clearly, how can we meaningfully influence society as salt and light?

Above all, we must focus on the kingdom to come, the kingdom that's our true home. Only by saturating ourselves in the reality of God's kingdom can we effectively live as salt and light in this earthly kingdom. Salt and light are preserving and illuminating. When we enter conversations about troubling issues with humility, grace, and kindness, we earn the right to be heard. Admitting that we don't know what we don't know isn't a sign of weakness but an opportunity to build a bridge across disagreement. Our actions should always be expressions of this prayer:

> *Your kingdom come.*
> *Your will be done*
> *on earth as it is in heaven.*
> **MATTHEW 6:10**

In what ways has this week's study led you to question some of your political assumptions?

PRAYER AND REFLECTION

Ask God to give you conviction and clarity as you engage in political dialogue and action. Thank the Holy Spirit for the grace to participate and the conviction to act.

ENGAGE WITH THE WORLD

The purpose of this section is to help you process key ideas from this week's study and think differently about the way you engage with the world. Take some time to thoughtfully consider the following questions. Then record your responses.

A Christian worldview should affect the way we see everything. We need Christians at all levels of society to function as salt and light, applying their God-given convictions in every societal sphere. Christians should influence education, health care, welfare and taxation policies, trade, and everything in between. Let me be very clear: I want to see Christians in our church getting involved in the political process. Some people may even be so passionate about political engagement that they pursue it as a calling. But for most of us, the following questions are good guidelines for discerning when we should and shouldn't get involved.

Are the facts so clear and the moral obligations so obvious that Christians, in good conscience, can't disagree with addressing this particular issue?

Does the issue rise to the level that our Christian witness requires us to speak?

About what issues of our day can you answer yes to both of the previous questions?

What might gospel-centered engagement on these issues look like?

GOSPEL
VICTORY

START

Welcome to group session 8 of Gospel Above All.

> **The past two weeks we've talked about complicated topics. What's one key takeaway form either of those weeks?**

> **Once you have determined to make something a priority, how do you keep it a priority?**

The gospel is our banner and our rallying point. I hope through this study you've seen that the gospel affects every area of the Christian life, from our personal spiritual journey, to our mission, to the way we live, and to the type of community we create. It's not enough to say the gospel is above all. We have to work to keep it above all. We have to commit to it in order to see gospel victory. That's what we will examine in this final week of study.

WATCH

Refer to this viewer guide as you watch video session 8.

If we confess _____, we are going to be _____.

When we confess the gospel faithfully, not only will Jesus _____ our church from Satan, but He will also enable us to _____ God's kingdom into Satan's most well-fortified strongholds.

The goal has always been _____—going forward in obedience and _____.

We need to take _____ for the sake of the _____.

Jesus is not _____ to just be Lord of the church as it exists right now. Jesus died to be Lord of the _____ earth.

Because of Jesus' promise that He puts on this confession, we will never be _____ when there's such _____ in our community and in our world.

Take Notes:

DISCUSS

Use the following questions to discuss the video teaching.

Read the following verses.

> [Jesus] asked them, "who do you say that I am?" Simon Peter
> answered, "You are the Messiah, the Son of the living God." Jesus
> responded, "Blessed are you, Simon son of Jonah because flesh
> and blood did not reveal this to you, but my Father in heaven.
> And I also say to you that you are Peter, and on this rock I will
> build my church, and the gates of Hades will not overpower it."
>
> **MATTHEW 16:15-18**

How does this passage help us realize the power we have in bold gospel confession?

Peter's confession that Jesus is the Messiah is the cornerstone of the church. For two millennia, the church has advanced by clinging to this confession as its organizing principle. Jesus promised that if we're faithful in our confession, then we'll be able to advance deeper and deeper into enemy territory. We'll be unstoppable if we "hold on to the confession of our hope without wavering, since he who promised is faithful" (Heb. 10:23).

> Whatever you ask in my name, I will do it so that the Father may be
> glorified in the Son. If you ask me anything in my name, I will do it.
>
> **JOHN 14:13-14**

Why should Jesus' willingness to give us what we ask in prayer lead us to take great risks for the kingdom? What keeps you from taking risks?

Any kingdom advancement comes with risk. That's why we pray. Jesus wants to glorify the Father. When we pray in accordance with that desire, Jesus will be faithful to answer our request. Therefore, we're ultimately secure, no matter what risk we take. Champions of the gospel have to get comfortable with risk.

Remember, Jesus isn't content to be Lord of the church as it exists right now. He died to be Lord of the entire earth. Why should this fact compel us to keep the gospel above all?

Do you tend to think of the whole world as Jesus' territory, or do you limit Him by the risks you don't take or by the prayers you don't pray?

Jesus has placed a promise on the confession of the gospel. We should never be satisfied when so many people are lost in our community and our world. The whole world is Jesus' territory. The church has received the power of heaven to bring the kingdom of heaven to bear on earth. This happens as we continue to elevate the gospel above all.

The purpose of this study has been to lead you to recommit to the gospel. What has most convicted and challenged you in these eight weeks of study?

RESPOND

Use these questions to apply today's teaching.

Based on the conviction you expressed, how will you continue to respond in the weeks to come?

PRAYER

Close the session by confessing the gospel together.

We confess that Jesus is the Lord of the whole earth, the King of kings and Lord of lords.

Jesus is the Messiah, the Christ, the Son of the living God, the one way of salvation for all people, the one name under heaven given to people whereby we must be saved. Whoever will call on the name of the Lord will be saved.

There's no difference between the Jew and the Greek, the black and the white, the rich and the poor, the Democrat and the Republican. Since the beginning of time, there's only been one race of human—sinner—and one Savior—Jesus.

The same Lord is Lord of all, bestowing His riches on whoever calls on Him. He's not willing that any should perish but that all should come to repentance.

We confess these truths because the Bible Jesus authorized teaches them and because all Scripture is given by the inspiration of God. Whether or not this confession is unpopular, it comes with the power of God, and that's the last thing we want to lose.

Remind group members to complete this week's personal study.

PRAY BOLDLY

I want to end our journey together with a call to prayer and a call to take risks in light of the gospel. Today we'll look at prayer, and the next personal study will be devoted to risks.

> **Read Luke 11:5-13. How closely does your prayer life match this teaching of Jesus?**

I think Jesus' first disciples must have found His teaching about prayer in Luke 11 as alarming as we do. That's one reason that just a few chapters later Jesus presented essentially the same teaching. We're so slow to believe what He said about praying with bold desperation that He repeated the lesson. But the second story is even more shocking than the first:

> *He told them a parable on the need for them to pray always and not give up. "There was a judge in a certain town who didn't fear God or respect people. And a widow in that town kept coming to him, saying, 'Give me justice against my adversary.' For a while he was unwilling, but later he said to himself, 'Even though I don't fear God or respect people, yet because this widow keeps pestering me, I will give her justice, so that she doesn't wear me out by her persistent coming.' "*
>
> **LUKE 18:1-5**

With whom are we meant to identity in this parable?

Unbelievably, Jesus concluded this parable by saying, in effect, "This is what it's like to pray to God." Here's the key to understanding parables. When you listen to a parable, you should be thinking, *Somebody in this parable represents me, and somebody in this parable represents God.* That's how parables work. So the disciples were listening and thinking, *OK, we have to be the needy old widow, right? But that would make God ... whoa, wait a minute. You're saying God is like a grumpy old judge who doesn't care about people or about justice and gave this woman what she wanted only because she was annoying him.* Who else but Jesus could get away with that analogy?

But the point here isn't to simply compare God to an unjust, uncaring judge. It's to contrast Him with one. Even an unjust judge will eventually grant a request because of our boldness. How much more, then, should we boldly approach our Heavenly Father who loves us?

Do you sometimes limit the intensity of your prayers? If so, why?

Why should our identity as God's children give us unparalleled boldness in prayer?

The woman in Luke 18 approached the judge as a stranger; we approach our God as beloved children. The judge in Jesus' story cared neither for justice nor for us, but our Judge cared so much about us that He climbed out of His Judge's chair and took the penalty of judgment Himself.

When we understand the character of God revealed by this contrast, we suddenly find that we can pray with startling boldness. You know who approaches me with more boldness than anyone else in my life? My kids. I can't count the number of times I've opened my eyes at three a.m. to one of my children saying, "I want some water."

Honestly, who else could get away with that? My kids approach me with undaunted confidence in my goodness toward them. That's precisely the way God wants us to approach Him. We're like children who are welcome to interrupt their daddy at any hour of the night, with whatever need we have.

What matter do you need to take to God right now with urgency?

In what sense do we limit the effectiveness of our prayers by refusing to be as bold as Jesus allows and expects us to be?

Jesus pressed this point in Luke 11:13, saying, "If you then, who are evil, know how to give good gifts to your children ..." *Evil* is a pretty dramatic word to use in this context, isn't it? Why did Jesus use it? Is it just another reminder of our depravity? Not really. Jesus called even our good parenting moments evil because, when compared to God's love for us, that's precisely the way they look. Even when I'm being the best dad I can possibly be, Jesus says God's love for His children is so superior that by comparison, my love could be classified as evil.

Think of how tenderly you love your kids. That's nothing compared to God's compassion for His children. Grasp this reality, and it will transform the requests you make of God. You'll enter His throne room with boldness, asking for great things and small things, just as your kids ask you.

What would your prayers for others look like if you really believed God has that kind of love for you and for the world?

Why not start praying those kinds of prayers this week, this day, or this very hour?

PRAYER AND REFLECTION

End your study today by praying the Lord's Prayer. Afterward ask God for radical boldness in gospel witness.

He said to them, "Whenever you pray, say,
Father, your name be honored as holy.
Your kingdom come.
Give us each day our daily bread.
And forgive us our sins,
for we ourselves also forgive everyone
in debt to us.
And do not bring us into temptation."
LUKE 11:2-4

ENGAGE WITH YOUR COMMUNITY

The purpose of this section is to help you process key ideas from this week's study with other members of your group. In light of what we've studied in this week's first personal study, meet together with a few other believers and pray with the boldness of a child. But before you do that, record all you want to request from God.

List all you want to pray for.

After you've met together and prayed, record the difference it made to pray together with other believers, aware of your common bond as children of God and as brothers and sisters in Christ.

BLESSED ARE THE RISK-TAKERS

How do you typically regard risk-takers? Are they commendable, crazy, or somewhere in between? Why?

Jesus once told a story that established risk-taking as a necessary component of true discipleship. It was about a rich boss who left behind sums of money for his servants to invest. To one servant he gave five talents; to another, two; to another, one. A talent was a rather large unit of money—about twenty years' salary (in our terms about a million dollars). So to one man he gave twenty years' salary; to another, double that; and to another, a hundred years' worth.

> *The man who had received five talents went, put them to work, and earned five more. In the same way the man with two earned two more. But the man who had received one talent went off, dug a hole in the ground, and hid his master's money.*
> **MATTHEW 25:16-18**

The man with two million turned it into four, and the man with five turned it into ten. When the master returned, he commended the first two servants for their wise investment of his resources. But to the one who did nothing he said:

> *You evil, lazy servant! If you knew that I reap where I haven't sown and gather where I haven't scattered, then you should have deposited my money with the bankers, and I would have received my money back with interest when I returned. So take the talent from him and give it to the one who has ten talents. For to everyone who has, more will be given, and he will have more than enough. But from the one who does not have, even what he has will be taken away from him. And throw this good-for-nothing servant into the outer darkness, where there will be weeping and gnashing of teeth.*
> **MATTHEW 25:26-30**

What shocks you about the way the master responded?

Jesus represents the master in this parable. By extension we are meant to see ourselves as the servants. Two points about that parable grip me.

1. Jesus commended the first two servants for taking a risk with His money. Investing it means they could have lost it. That's the nature of investing: no guarantees! Yet Jesus didn't say, "What were you thinking? You could have lost all My money!" Instead, he commended them.

2. The second point that stands out is even more startling. Jesus called the one who didn't take the risk wicked. What had he done? There seemed to be no stealing, immorality, or even reckless irresponsibility involved. He didn't waste the master's money on partying, prostitutes, gambling, or first-class accommodations in the Caribbean. In fact, he hadn't spent a single penny on himself. He returned 100 percent of what he had been given to the master. And for that Jesus called him wicked.

How does this parable challenge your understanding of what it means to be wicked?

Do you ever wonder what character quality separated the first two servants in Jesus' parable from the third? In other words, why were they able to risk for the master when the third one couldn't? We find a clue in the way the third servant responded to the master:

> The man who had received one talent also approached and said, "Master, I know you. You're a harsh man, reaping where you haven't sown and gathering where you haven't scattered seed. So I was afraid and went off and hid your talent in the ground. See, you have what is yours."
> **MATTHEW 25:24-25**

The third servant didn't trust his master's goodness. Apparently, the other two servants knew their Master was gracious, as well as competent enough to handle any mistakes they made in pursuing their risk.

Every great risk in God's name begins with confidence in His goodness and trustworthiness. Our God is so good, gracious, and powerful that we can never ask or assume too much of Him. We don't offend Him with large requests; we offend Him with small ones. John Newton, the writer of the hymn "Amazing Grace," expressed that reality this way:

> *Thou art coming to a King,*
> *Large petitions with thee bring;*
> *For his grace and power are such,*
> *None can ever ask too much.*[1]

We have a Master who has not only commanded us to risk but has also promised us that as we do so, led by His Spirit, He will multiply our investments in the harvest of His kingdom.

What's your one key takeaway from this study? How will it help you keep the gospel above all?

What's one big risk you need to take for the sake of the gospel in the world?

PRAYER AND REFLECTION

Spend time asking God what risk you need to take. Ask Him to show you what God-sized gospel adventure He's calling you to. Pray for boldness and confidence to walk forward in obedience, knowing God will always supply everything you need to do what He asks.

1. John Newton, "Come, My Soul, Thy Suit Prepare," *Liturgy and Hymns for the Use of the Protestant Church of the United Brethren, or Moravians* (Bethelem, PA: Moravian Publication Office, 1866), 194.

ENGAGE WITH THE WORLD

The purpose of this section is to help you process key ideas from this week's study and think differently about the way you engage with the world. Take some time to thoughtfully consider the following questions. Then record your responses.

We serve a God for whom risk is required. Our church has asked God to allow us to plant one thousand churches and bless one thousand cities by 2050. We want to send out five thousand people as church-planting teams. We've started a school to train pastors and church leaders. We've asked God to let us baptize fifty thousand people in the Raleigh-Durham area. We've asked Him to let us be part of major awakenings in Muslim and European nations. Each year we try to give away more money and send out more leaders than we feel we can afford. Only when our giving scares us do we know we're getting close to the target.

Some well-meaning people have called our vision grandiose; others, foolish. However, we believe it embodies the required faithfulness to the Master who entrusted us with a small pile of talents to invest until He returns. He's gracious enough to compensate for our incompetence, and we believe He would rather have us risk too much than play it too safe.

In what way do you need to take a risk? Is the Spirit of God leading you to share Christ with a friend, go on a mission trip, or walk across the street to knock on the neighbor's door?

What steps will you take to pursue this risk?

LEADER GUIDE

Welcome students to Session 1 of *Gospel Above All*, provide study books, and give an overview of the topics addressed in this Bible study.

SESSION 1 *Gospel Above All*

Start (Optional)

As an icebreaker, play a game of "Would You Rather?" with your group. Ask the following questions and instruct them to answer by raising their hands when you read their preferred response.

- Would you rather lose your money and possessions or every picture you've ever taken?
- Would you rather spend your whole life in a perfect virtual reality or in real life?

Each of these statements requires students to prioritize. Use this activity to help them understand the importance of our devotion to the gospel above all else.

Group Discussion

Use the Watch section on page 10 to take notes as you watch the video for Session 1. Then use the content and questions on pages 11-13 to discuss the video session.

As You Go

Remind students to complete the Personal Studies on pages 14-21. Then, close your group time by using the prayer prompt on page 13.

Notes

SESSION 2 *Gospel Change*

Start (Optional)

Ask students to think back to the first thing they wanted to be "when they grow up." Then ask them how they have grown since then and how that idea has changed over time. Just as we constantly grow physically and emotionally, we also grow spiritually through a process called sanctification. Help them understand how the gospel applies not only to the moment of their salvation but also to their daily lives.

Group Discussion

Use the Watch section on page 24 to take notes as you watch the video for Session 2. Then use the content and questions on pages 25-27 to discuss the video session.

As You Go

Remind students to complete the Personal Studies on pages 28-35. Then, close your group time by using the prayer prompt on page 27.

Notes

. . . .
. . . .
. . . .

SESSION 3 *Gospel Mission*

Start (Optional)

Place students in pairs to create Blind Drawings. Give one person in each pair a piece of paper and pencil, and instruct them to sit back-to-back. Give one person an object or scene, which they must describe to their partner without using obvious words as the partner draws the scene as described. Then the pair reveals the drawing to see how accurate the drawing is. Use this activity to illustrate how important communication is, especially when it comes to sharing the gospel. It isn't enough just for us to know the truth; we have to tell it as well.

Group Discussion

Use the Watch section on page 38 to take notes as you watch the video for Session 3. Then use the content and questions on pages 39-41 to discuss the video session.

As You Go

Remind students to complete the Personal Studies on pages 42-49. Then, close your group time by using the prayer prompt on page 41.

Notes

. . . .
. . . .
. . . .

SESSION 4 *Gospel Evangelism*

Start (Optional)

This session focuses on evangelism, a word that can be overwhelming no matter your age. Give each student a piece of paper and a pen, and ask them to write out their testimony. Then, ask if any students feel comfortable sharing their testimony aloud. If so, allow a few minutes for sharing before you dig into this week's study.

Group Discussion

Use the Watch section on page 52 to take notes as you watch the video for Session 4. Then use the content and questions on pages 53-55 to discuss the video session.

As You Go

Remind students to complete the Personal Studies on pages 56-63. Then, close your group time by using the prayer prompt on page 55.

Notes

. . . .
. . . .
. . . .

SESSION 5 *Gospel Grace*

Start (Optional)

Instruct students to think about someone they know who is full of grace.
Then ask:
- What have you learned from them?
- How can their example help you better understand the gift of forgiveness?

Just as God has shown us grace and forgiveness, we are called to show grace and forgiveness to others.

Group Discussion

Use the Watch section on page 66 to take notes as you watch the video for Session 5. Then use the content and questions on pages 67-69 to discuss the video session.

As You Go

Remind students to complete the Personal Studies on pages 70-77. Then, close your group time by using the prayer prompt on page 69.

Notes

. . . .

. . . .

. . . .

SESSION 6 *Gospel Community*

Start (Optional

Bring in a large map of the world or smaller printed copies of a world map for each student. Tell students to point to different areas of the map and give one fact about the culture there. Tally how many different countries students mention. Then, talk about different nationalities and cultures that are common in your own area. Although this week's topic can be a sensitive one, you can encourage students to recognize and appreciate different cultures around them.

Group Discussion

Use the Watch section on page 80 to take notes as you watch the video for Session 6. Then use the content and questions on pages 81-83 to discuss the video session.

As You Go

Remind students to complete the Personal Studies on pages 84-91. Then, close your group time by using the prayer prompt on page 83.

Notes

. . . .

. . . .

. . . .

SESSION 7 *Gospel Unity*

Start (Optional)

Although students may not be able to vote yet, the church has a responsibility to teach them a godly approach to thinking about and engaging with politics. Before you begin the session, it might be a good idea to see how much your group knows already. The point isn't to tell students what to believe or how to vote, but to become more thoughtful and intentional about the way they engage with the political process.

Group Discussion

Use the Watch section on page 94 to take notes as you watch the video for Session 7. Then use the content and questions on pages 95-97 to discuss the video session.

As You Go

Remind students to complete the Personal Studies on pages 98-105. Then, close your group time by using the prayer prompt on page 97.

Notes

. . . .

. . . .

. . . .

SESSION 8 *Gospel Victory*

Start (Optional)

Review the main points of the previous weeks of study and allow students an opportunity to share ways this study has affected their understanding and expressions of the gospel. Ask: *What changes do you intend to make in your lives to place a greater emphasis on the gospel?*

Group Discussion

Use the Watch section on page 108 to take notes as you watch the video for Session 8. Then use the content and questions on pages 109-111 to discuss the video session.

As You Go

Remind students to complete the Personal Studies on pages 112-119. Then, close your group time by using the prayer prompt on page 111.

- Since this is the last week of your study, encourage members to complete the form on page 126-127 as a way of reflecting on this study.
- If you're providing Bible-study books for your next study together, distribute them at the end of this session.

Notes

STUDY START DATE

_____ / _____ / _____

✎ **Record a few details about this season of your life.**

FAMILY |

_____ _____
name   age

_____ _____

_____ _____

_____ _____

EDUCATION |

_____
school

_____
grade

HOME |

_____
city   state

What do you hope to get out of this study?

Mark your spiritual temperature.

hot

cold

💡 **MAJOR EVENTS IN THE WORLD** |

_____

_____

📍 **KEY ISSUES IN YOUR WORLD** |

_____

_____

STUDY END DATE

_____ / _____ / _____

★ **TOP FIVE FAVORITE POINTS FROM THIS STUDY**

page #

_____

_____

_____

_____

_____

**WHERE DID
YOU STUDY?**

○ **Home**

○ **Church**

○ **Another home:**
_____

○ **Other:**
_____

**WITH WHOM DID YOU
DO THIS STUDY?**

_____

_____

_____

_____

**WITH WHOM DO
YOU WANT TO SHARE
THIS STUDY?**

_____

──── **BIBLE VERSES TO MEMORIZE** ────